How often has even a sm[___] a big problem in your rel[___] workers, your clients or cust[___]? How helpful would it have be[___]l communication coach by your side?

Now, FORTUNE 500 consultant Beverly Inman-Ebel's positive approach shows you how to

- Make people feel important by mastering the art of listening

- Get people to open up by using six powerful techniques

- Eliminate the communication "trouble words" from your conversation

- Create your own "public and private attitude plans" to better manage your communication and your environment

- Give compliments that change the way people act

- Give corrections that leave people feeling stronger and willing to change

- Read "body talk" and listen for the "secrets of the voice"

- Reduce conflict and stress by recognizing and communicating effectively with each of the four primary behavioral styles

Whether you are a manager, an employee, a business owner, a professional, or a parent, this insightful, information-packed book offers a powerful toolkit to help you communicate more effectively at work and at home — and live a richer, happier life!

Praise for *Talk Is NOT Cheap!*

"**I**f you're a woman who's serious about business, you definitely need this book. *Talk Is NOT Cheap!* is one valuable tool you can put in your toolkit to make you even more competitive — and the skills it teaches you will improve all aspects of your life."

Phyllis Hill-Slater
Vice President, Les Femmes Chefs D'Entreprises Mondiales
Past President, National Association of Women Business Owners

"**I**deal for anyone looking to become a better communicator. It's a blend of psychology and management theory, written in plain language, using simple analogies designed to help people in everday interactions."

ForeWord Magazine

"**I**n *Talk Is NOT Cheap!* Beverly Inman-Ebel shows how to set your own attitude and 'altitude,' the communicative value of listening more than you talk, how to find a better way to express what you want to say, and the value of treating others the way they want to be treated. An invaluable tutorial and guide."

The Midwest Book Review

TALK IS NOT CHEAP!

SAVING THE HIGH COST OF MISUNDERSTANDING AT WORK AND HOME

Talk Is NOT Cheap!

Saving the High Cost of Misunderstanding at Work and Home

BY

Beverly Inman-Ebel
MA, CCC-SLP

Bard Press

Austin, Texas

TALK IS NOT CHEAP!
Saving the High Cost of Misunderstanding at Work and Home
Copyright © 1999 by Beverly Inman-Ebel. All rights reserved.

Bard Press
1515 Capital of Texas Highway S., Suite 107
Austin, TX 78746
512-329-8373 voice, 512-329-6051 fax
www.bardpress.com

Ordering Information
To order additional copies, contact your local bookstore or call 800-945-3132. Quantity discounts are available.

ISBN 1-885167-33-4 trade paperback, 1-885167-34-2 hardcover

Library of Congress Cataloging-in-Publication Data
Inman-Ebel, Beverly, 1951-
    Talk is not cheap! : saving the high cost of misunderstanding at work and home / by Beverly Inman-Ebel.
        p.   cm.
    Includes bibliographical references and index.
    ISBN 1-885167-34-2 (hardcover). -- ISBN 1-885167-33-4 (pbk.)
    1. Miscommunication   2. Interpersonal communication.   3. Business communication.   4. Interpersonal relations. I. Title.
BF637.C45I54 1999
153.6--dc21   99-12263
                                                                      CIP

The author may be contacted at the following address:

Beverly Inman-Ebel
TLC, Talk Listen Communicate, LLC
842 South Germantown Road
Chattanooga, TN 37412
1-888-BECAUSE
Fax: 423-624-4365
E-mail: tlc@byac.com
Website: www.byac.com

Credits
Editor: Jeff Morris
Proofreaders: Deborah Costenbader, Laurie Drummond
Index: Linda Webster
Cover design: Suzanne Pustejovsky
Text design/production: Jeff Morris
Illustration: Terri Ebel
Art direction: Suzanne Pustejovsky

First printing: March 1999
Second printing: August 1999
Third printing: January 2000

This book is dedicated to my parents,
Clancy and Charlotte Inman,
who gave me the right proportions of roots and
wings, and instilled in me the conviction
that I could do anything I set my mind to do.

CONTENTS

ABOUT THE AUTHOR

Beverly Inman-Ebel is a speech-language pathologist with a special interest in effective adult interaction. As founder and CEO of TLC, Talk Listen Communicate, LLC, Beverly and

her staff work with companies, organizations, and individuals to achieve permanent and positive change in behavior. This is accomplished through corporate cultural coaching and individual and small group training.

Beverly, a member of the National Speakers Association, speaks at national and state conventions and for corporations nationwide. She has received national attention in the *Wall Street Journal, USA Today, Time, Glamour,* and *Success* magazines, and on *CBS Evening News* and *ABC World News* for her work with voice and communication improvement for business image. The American Speech-Language-Hearing Association gave her its Public Information Exchange Award for her work with an ABC affiliate station producing regular features on effective communication. Beverly has authored numerous articles under the title "Communication Please" for Meridian Publishing Company of Ogden, Utah.

Beverly participated in a White House conference and reception on brain development and learning with President and Mrs. Clinton. She has traveled with the United States Department of Commerce to South Africa to establish trade between the two nations. Since 1996 Beverly has served on the Tennessee Governor's Task Force on Women Business Owners. She was chosen as the 1998 recipient of the Jane Cosby Henderson Woman of Achievement award.

Beverly received her bachelor of science in speech and hearing science with high honors and her master of arts in speech language pathology from the University of Tennessee. She also received postgraduate certification in Silva Mind Control in Laredo, Texas, and Myo Functional Therapy in Coral Gables, Florida.

Beverly Inman-Ebel can be contacted by

- phone: 888-BECAUSE
- fax: 423-624-4365
- e-mail: tlc@byac.com
- website: www.byac.com

ACKNOWLEDGMENTS

I thank Terri Ebel, who created the illustrations and spent many hours teaching through her art; David Rodney Fraley, who encouraged me to write and kept bugging me until I did it; and my dear friend Therese Padgett, who saw me through the questioning times, was my brainstorm partner, and helped me to focus.

I thank the following people, who read my manuscript and gave me priceless feedback: Bill Bosworth, Vice President and General Manager, Knoxville Division of Coca-Cola Enterprises, Knoxville, Tennessee; Caryn Colgan, St. Louis, Missouri; Linda Frazier, Director of Marketing, Masland Carpets, Inc., Mobile, Alabama; Gary John, Dallas, Texas; Debra Johnston, Director, The Coca-Cola Company, Atlanta, Georgia; Mart Kilpatrick, Atlanta; Bob Lehmann, Director of Risk Management, Coca-Cola Enterprises, Atlanta; Kay Scott, CEO, Planned Parenthood of Georgia, Atlanta; Phyllis Scott, Executive Assistant to General Manager, Rusch, Inc., Duluth, Georgia; Catherine Smith, Signal Mountain, Tennessee; George Smith, Divisional President, Dixie Group, Inc., Chattanooga, Tennessee; James S. Smith, Vice President Administration, Lanier Worldwide, Atlanta; Pat St. Charles, Treasurer, Citizen's Savings and Loan, Chattanooga.

I thank my many clients, who provided me with life's experiences and who taught me much. I am grateful to Bard Press and all the talented people associated with it, including Ray Bard, Jeff Morris, and Suzanne Pustejovsky.

I thank my sons, Tye and Logan, who did without their mom many days so I could write and edit.

Finally, I thank my husband, Ken Ebel, for his support and guidance, and for being my partner in this project and in life.

It isn't that they can't see the solution.
It's that they can't see the problem.

G. K. CHESTERTON

THE HIGH COST
OF MISUNDERSTANDING

alk is cheap!" You've heard that more than a few times, haven't you? You've probably said it to yourself or to someone else, or at least thought it a time or two. Do you think it's true? Consider the following cases.

Misunderstanding No. 1: A disgruntled employee confides to the manager of human resources that many of his fellow workers think the company is not being fair to the work force; word is that a union representative had promised better working conditions, higher wages, and more generous benefits. The HR manager listens, considers it just talk, and takes no action.

Cost: Within three months a union campaign costs the corporation millions of dollars. The HR manager loses her job.

Misunderstanding No. 2: With two days left in the month, an eager salesperson struggles to help his sales center meet its quota. He goes to one of his more dependable accounts and, talking excitedly, persuades the buyer to take delivery of 500 cases of two-liter soft drinks. He becomes the hero of the day. When the drinks are delivered, however, he receives a disturbing call from his customer: "Not five hundred cases — five hundred bottles!"

Cost: Time runs out; the sales center misses its quota; the customer is unhappy. The sales hero becomes the villain.

Misunderstanding No. 3: A corporate vice president hears an unfounded rumor about a senior manager he knows well. Upset and concerned about a possible ethical lapse, the VP calls the manager to his office and reminds him that accepting expensive gifts from clients is prohibited. The manager denies having received any presents. The VP responds, "Everyone knows you like nice things."

Cost: The manager feels he has been pronounced guilty without a trial. The VP regrets his careless remark and apologizes, but the manager goes away angry. The relationship between the two is permanently impaired. The manager's entire department gets caught up in the tension. Productivity falls, teamwork vanishes, and the manager is eventually relieved of his duties.

Misunderstanding No. 4: A husband and wife are excited about their project, using their woodworking tools to make Christmas presents for family and friends. One Saturday, while the husband goes to get more wood, the wife takes great pride in sanding the constructed pieces. On his way home, the husband narrowly avoids colliding with a careless driver. Still seething with anger, he enters the workshop and sees his wife's handiwork. He scolds her: "Why didn't you use the thousand-grit sandpaper? You should have known better. Now we'll have to redo all of these."

Cost: The wife's enthusiasm for the project dwindles. She busies herself with other tasks and stops coming to the workshop. The husband, realizing his mistake, tries to apologize. He feels guilty; she feels worthless. They end up buying last-minute gifts that satisfy neither.

The consequences of misunderstanding, as you can see, are not cheap. They range from hurt feelings to ruined relationships to long-lasting, incalculable economic penalties. Talk is, after all, not cheap.

WHAT PRICE MISUNDERSTANDING?

Communication is not perfect. Even under the best of circumstances, we frequently fail to get across our own ideas or we fall short of understanding what others are trying to tell us. And we always pay a price — sometimes small, sometimes large. Think back to your most recent misunderstanding. What did it cost you to correct it?

We shrug and say, misunderstandings are inevitable. We just have to learn to live with them and write off the cost.

Now I'm going to say something clear, bold, and unequivocal:

Baloney.

I say that misunderstandings are not inevitable. I say that we can communicate in such a way that misunderstandings can be eliminated. And that by eliminating misunderstandings, we can save in many different ways:

- Businesses can save money.
- Managers can save time.
- People can save relationships.
- The individual can save self-esteem.

I've even written a book about it — this one.

Talk is not cheap! When we devalue our communication, we pay the high costs that misunderstandings bring. We can save money, time, relationships, and self-esteem by investing wisely in this valuable resource.

It is a luxury to be understood.

RALPH WALDO EMERSON

MAKING DEPOSITS WITH PEOPLE

Think of the relationship you have with another person as a checking account. On a regular basis you deposit funds into your account because you know you'll be writing checks or making withdrawals. It is in your best interest to keep a positive balance in your account. The consequence of failing to do this is to pay a fee and lose credibility.

In your relationships with people at work and home, you may have to correct their behavior, postpone listening, or in some way disappoint them. These are the withdrawals in your account with them. Misunderstandings are more insidious. They are like automatic bank drafts; you may not immediately realize that the funds have been removed. To avoid unintentional overdrafts and ensure that your account balance stays positive, you need to make regular deposits.

FOUR DEPOSITS FOR BALANCE

There are four deposits that you need to make regularly to maintain a positive balance in your people account. These deposits are the principles upon which we all communicate with ourselves and one another.

FIRST DEPOSIT: SET YOUR OWN ATTITUDE AND ALTITUDE

Eleanor Roosevelt said, "No one can take your dreams from you, except you." The first deposit is one that you make to yourself. What you say to yourself is the foundation for what you are able to say to others. When you make limiting or negative statements to yourself, or when you replay in your mind a harmful message someone else has given you, you cannot maintain your balance, because you are teetering to maintain your own self-esteem.

Guilt and worry keep you unbalanced. You cannot control what another person says and does, but you can control what you do with that information. When you take charge of your own attitude, you are unstoppable. Your altitude, or net worth, is determined by your attitude. Invest in yourself. You're worth it!

Second Deposit: Listen More Than You Talk

One of the greatest gifts you can give cannot be wrapped in foil paper and satin bows. It is the gift of time — the time you spend listening to others. This gift is one of the greatest deposits you can make into your people account.

If you take the letters in "listen" and rearrange them, you can make the word "silent." You must be silent to truly listen. You must silence your thoughts, questions, and preconceived notions to begin to understand what the other person is trying to say. This deposit can, almost by itself, eliminate misunderstanding. Invest in other people. Listen to them! God gave us two ears and one mouth. Do you think there might have been a divine plan in this?

Third Deposit: Find a Better Way to Say It

This deposit requires planning. There is always a better way to give sensitive information. Too often, though, we blurt out our thoughts without thinking them through. Our fast mouth betrays us and creates misunderstanding, a liability to our account balance. We realize our mistake and strive to fix it, only to compound the error. After a few ill-planned attempts, we give up, perhaps blaming the other person. Save time and relationships by auditing your words before you bankrupt yourself!

Fourth Deposit: Treat Others the Way They Want to Be Treated

Here's a slight twist on the Golden Rule (I don't think God would be offended). Since we're all different, it makes sense that the other person may not want what you want. For a job well done, you may want the spotlight with your deed mentioned in the company newsletter. The other guy may consider that hype and prefer a handwritten note of appreciation. When you travel to another country, you have to exchange currency. When you make deposits to others, make sure it's in the currency they can use!

The Four Deposits for Balance, when credited to your account, will eliminate the high cost of misunderstandings at work and home. Your equity will be priceless!

LOOKING AHEAD

The rest of this book gives you a detailed plan to eliminate misunderstandings through the use of the Four Deposits for

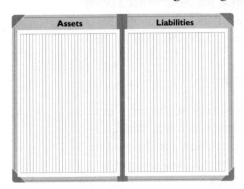

Balance. At the end of each chapter you will find a "ledger" listing "assets" and "liabilities." The "assets" are actions you can take to increase your "balance"; the "liabilities" are actions you should avoid in order not to decrease it.

Read; ponder; apply. Be prepared to change your life.

Excellence is achieved by the mastery of fundamentals.

VINCE LOMBARDI

FIRST DEPOSIT

SET YOUR OWN ATTITUDE AND ALTITUDE

FIRST DEPOSIT:
SET YOUR OWN ATTITUDE
AND ALTITUDE

If something is wrong, fix it. Train yourself
not to worry. Worry never fixes anything.

MARY HEMINGWAY

GETTING TO KNOW
YOUR INNER SELF

he first deposit in
Four Deposits for Bal-
ance is this: Set your
own attitude and alti-
tude. Attitude can be determined by what we believe to
be true. It not only affects our mood, it can determine our
health. Why is a communication specialist interested in
attitude? Attitude is what we say to ourselves, or
intracommunication. It is the foundation for all external

O ne winter day during graduate school, my friend and I were building a snowdog (the creative person's version of a snowman) when my artistic talents took a military turn. After exchanging countless snowballs with my co-sculptor, I gasped in horror, "Oh, no! My feet got wet and now I'm going to get strep throat!"

My friend laughed and said, "That's one of the craziest things I've ever heard you say!" I was still trying to impress this guy, so I took the rebuke seriously. I recited my medical history: the many times I had suffered a sore throat after getting my feet wet in chilly weather.

"The problem isn't in your feet," he said, "it's in your head!" With slushy boots and injured pride, I stomped up the stairs to my apartment.

That night before falling asleep, I began to have doubts. Maybe I wasn't being very logical after all. I would stay well, I decided. The next morning, I awoke, swallowed, and felt gloriously normal. I also felt quite superior to my former self. Where could I possibly have picked up such a notion?

Twelve years later, my snowdog partner and I had married and were busy raising two active preschool boys. One March weekend my parents came to visit. It was a cool rainy afternoon and the boys wanted to play outside. Anxious to get the house noise level down to 70 decibels, I consented and dressed them for the weather. My parents gave them affectionate hugs and, to my amazement, a warning: "Keep your feet dry or you'll get a sore throat!"

communication, what we say to others. Attitude affects our relationships, careers, and peace with self. To have balance with yourself and others, you must first get acquainted with your inner self.

ATTITUDE AND THE MIND

To gain a better understanding of yourself, it is important to understand how your mind works. The brain, the physical housing for the mind, is divided into two hemispheres: left and right.

LEFT HEMISPHERE

Your left hemisphere is the logical part of your mind. It stores your vocabulary, mathematical concepts, and most of the information you need for your working day.

It gives you advice. You know that little voice inside your head? The one that tells you not to pull out in front of the oncoming truck because it's closer than you think? Advice from your left hemisphere is important to consider; it can save your life. However, because it is based on your previous experiences, if you always listen to it, it can limit your life.

Your left hemisphere is not always "on." It didn't turn on for the first time until you were five to seven years old. Your logic and your advisor were asleep for the first several years of your life. That shouldn't be too surprising. How else can you explain kids believing in a fat, white-bearded little man climbing down (and up) a dirty chimney, bringing presents that certainly wouldn't fit the narrow opening? Per- 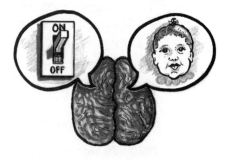 haps the best part is that flying reindeer (not geese, swans, or ducks) brought him to your house! Yet believe you did. Why? Because someone told you so, and at that age you had no mental defenses to advise you otherwise.

When my sons were six and five, they came to me to learn the truth about Santa Claus. They had asked before, but this time they specifically wanted to know whether it was true that Santa wore a red suit and slipped down the chimney. I asked, "Are you sure you want my opinion?" Yes, they did. After their left hemispheres got the bad news, the youngest one clapped his hands over his ears and walked away saying, "Don't tell me about the Easter Bunny! I don't want to know."

Perhaps I was up front early with my kids because of dubious information I got from my older sister when I was about their age. She told me there were snakes and alligators under our bed. When I finally got my nerve up to look down there and found none, she explained, in a tone that reminded me what a silly, pesky sister I was, that they only came out after dark. Before I graduated from high school — yes, long before — I realized she was having fun at my expense. Yet to this day, if I wake up with an arm hanging over the edge of a bed, I jerk it back onto the safety of the mattress, then remember I'm being silly.

Messages we receive in our early years, before the left hemisphere kicks in, stay with us. Perhaps science has recently discovered why the familiar verse from Proverbs holds such truth: "Bring up a child in the way he should go, and he will not soon depart from it."

RIGHT HEMISPHERE

The right hemisphere is the creative part of the brain. It controls some of the more intuitive communication functions, such as body language and tone of voice. It is the gateway to memory and long-term storage, the key to attitude. Many people do not demonstrate conscious control of their right hemisphere.

Right now, as you read this book, your right hemisphere is taking note of the lighting, the texture of your chair or bed, the air temperature, background noises, and objects in your peripheral vision. Are you conscious of all of this information that is entering your memory? Until the words on this page brought them to your attention, you probably weren't. The right hemisphere records in visual images, not in words. It records all your sensory input: visual, auditory, smell, taste, touch, and movement. Sometimes you'll hear a song and it will take you back to a particular

> Messages we receive in our early years, before the left hemisphere kicks in, stay with us.

time in your life. Or perhaps a certain aroma will remind you of your grandmother's kitchen when you were a child.

The sense of smell, directly connected to your limbic system, can easily stir your emotions. For instance, the smell of pine may make you feel industrious. No wonder we work ourselves into a frenzy during the Christmas holidays! The scent of lavender can make you feel very calm and relaxed. Citrus smells, such as lemon and orange, can make you feel happy. Keep some lemons in your refrigerator and chop them up in your garbage disposal the next time you are depressed!

The right hemisphere is gullible; it will believe anything you tell it when the left hemisphere, your protector, is off duty. We know the formative years of our childhood were unprotected, but now that we are adults, how do our minds work? The right hemisphere flies solo when you're ill with the flu or a cold, whenever you exercise, and during either the first thirty minutes after you awake or the last thirty minutes before you fall asleep. If you're a morning person, waking up ready to function and take on the world, then your right hemisphere works alone in the half hour before you fall asleep at night. If you wake up asleep like me, then you have about thirty minutes in the morning before your left hemisphere joins you.

A plant department manager was awakened at two a.m. by a telephone call from a third-shift supervisor. Line one was down due to a problem with the filling tube. The supervisor proposed moving the container cases to line three for fill-up at the beginning of the first shift. The department manager agreed, hung up, and went back to sleep. Upon arriving at the office at six a.m., he was furious at the idiot who had moved the cases instead of calling maintenance to clear the filling tube. He had a large serving of humble pie when he was reminded of his "half-brained" consent hours earlier.

Because your uncritical right hemisphere is left to its own devices, you should be careful what you do at these crucial moments. Watching the news, reading a scary book, or making a major decision may not be advisable. It's like driving: sometimes you need both hands on the steering wheel.

The right hemisphere is always turned on. If it shuts down, you're in big trouble. That is, you're in a deep coma, or dead. Wow! Put these characteristics together! Your right hemisphere controls attitude and bodily functions; it will believe anything you tell it (especially when the left hemisphere is down); and it's always there for you. What would happen if you told the right hemisphere a bunch of good stuff while the left side was taking a snooze? That has been a question of interest for the last two decades, and has brought some amazing answers.

●●●●●●●●●●●●●●●●●

POSITIVE VS. NEGATIVE THINKING

In preparation for the 1980 Olympics in Lake Placid, the United States Ski Team practiced going down the slopes and then spent hours each day mentally practicing the same route. They would relax, which turns the left hemisphere off, and imagine they were skiing. If they fell down, they mentally picked up themselves and did it again. Result? They won a bronze medal.

This method of imagining success is called Visual Motor Practice. It works because the gullible right hemisphere, which controls the body, doesn't know the difference between "I'm really skiing" and "I'm pretending I'm skiing." I've used it many times, as you may have, sometimes without even realizing it.

I love to garden in my courtyard. I often enter this haven of tranquillity at dawn when the world is quiet and cool. As the sun peeks over the mountains to the east, the birds will find me digging, pulling, and humming. Along with my love of gardening, however, comes an extreme dislike for bugs and snakes. One morning I found a black snake in one of the flower beds. I thought it was black; it was hard to tell under the predawn sky. Mind you, I didn't care what color it was. I froze with fear. My first instinct was to scream, "Ken!" But two things stopped me. First, I knew he was asleep; more important, the last time he tried to catch a snake he used a dirt rake, and the slithering creature escaped through the tines.

Adrenaline was pumping through my veins — fight or flight? I chose to fight. Backing away, I ran to the garden house and secured the ax. With pounding heart I raised the ax over my head and brought it down in a deadly arc. The deed was done. I had managed to cut my new 100-foot black garden hose neatly in two.

At first I was relieved, then a little chagrined at my previous fear. Then I did what any sane person would do — I sank to my knees and laughed. I imagined it was a snake, so my gullible right hemisphere reacted accordingly.

Researchers have studied the theory that, as far as your right hemisphere is concerned, seeing is believing. Athletes are usually good subjects because they are young and healthy, so several from various sports were asked to relax and imagine they were participating in their activities. Electrodes were hooked up to their muscles. The collected data revealed that the athletes' muscles contracted much as they would if they were actually going for a touchdown, dribbling a basketball, or playing whatever sport they imagined playing.

Our right hemisphere, which controls our body, doesn't know the meaning of reality.

What does this mean to us? It means our right hemisphere, the side that reads and controls the orientation of our body, doesn't know the meaning of reality. That is a powerful thought.

In other studies, professional actors were asked to donate blood samples before and after performing. When they played the role of a hero or heroine — you know, the good guy who saves the world — endorphins were found in their blood. Endorphins are substances the body makes and releases into the circulatory system that bring feelings of euphoria and great energy. When the same actors played the role of the villain, no endorphins were found. Now, what does this mean for you in the world of business? It means you don't have to be a hero — just believe you're good or pretend you're an asset. The endorphins you produce will give you additional energy, so you might just end up doing something wonderful after all!

One of the biggest problems in our society is the abuse of both legal and illegal drugs. Help me spread the word that people can get high on positive thoughts! If you're a skeptic, try this exercise. Imagine yourself successful in a particular event of your life. See it in your mind. Hear people congratulating you. Feel the emotion. Enjoy the moment. Review this "mental movie" every time you have a troubling thought.

There's no need to reach for a bottle or a cigarette. Reach within your mind for the help you seek.

There's no need to reach for a bottle or a cigarette. Reach within your mind for the help you seek.

In his book *Anatomy of an Illness,* Norman Cousins wrote about the power of positive thoughts. He was diagnosed with a fatal and rare disease. His doctors couldn't help him, but Cousins refused to give up. He started his own form of therapy. He surrounded himself with positive thoughts, words, and sights. He saw only people who would support him. He read only positive and uplifting material. He rented comical videos and laughed until he cried. Norm called laughter "jogging of the soul." What was the result of all this positive bombardment? He got better. You might say he laughed away his disease.

Dr. Bernie Siegel, in his book *Love, Medicine, and Miracles,* also confirmed the power of positive thoughts. As an oncologist, Dr. Siegel became curious why some of his cancer patients recovered while others with similar symptoms did not. After studying his patients, Dr. Siegel

SET YOUR OWN ATTITUDE AND ALTITUDE

discovered that patients with positive attitudes remained healthier. Many put their cancer in remission.

Parade magazine surveyed fifteen people who had lived HIV positive for many years but had not become ill. They all professed to be positive fanatics.

In my school cafeteria was a sign: "You are what you eat." In our homes and offices there should be one that reads, "You are what you say!"

I am a person who juggles several agendas at one time. In order to do so, I prioritize. One phrase I often used was "I'll put that on the back burner," meaning that agenda was not a high priority and could wait. For years, I've had difficulty with my back from time to time. Blame it on doing too much, lack of regular exercise, or just being a klutz, I was often seen donning a brace or at least moving stiffly. One day an observant friend recommended that I omit the "back burner" phrase from my vocabulary. I was skeptical but figured I had nothing to lose except some lower back pain. Guess what? I had fewer incidences of my back "burning" with pain after I quit using that reference. Now, some people would say it was all in my head in the first place. No argument here. I believe quite firmly that I am what I say, which means I now choose my words more carefully.

During the early twentieth century, a scientist by the name of Nikola Tesla was considered both a genius and a social recluse. He seldom granted interviews, but on one rare occasion he was asked how he invented items without ever making a mistake. He explained that he got an idea in his mind, developed it, and mentally "used" the item until it malfunctioned. Next, he would fix the error in his mind and then start the process over. Finally, when it was perfected in his mind, he would recreate it in the physical world and find immediate success.

What can you create in your mental laboratory that will bring success to you? Thoughts are not idle. Make yours work for, not against, you. Your attitude can indeed determine your altitude. Make yours positive.

O ne family vacation was a disaster. It seemed that everything that could go wrong did. The family consisted of my parents, parents-in-law, husband, children, sister, brother-in-law, nieces, and nephews. By midweek I was in a back brace and couldn't move my head to either side. I caught my reflection in the mirror of the condo we were renting. I looked pretty miserable. I straightened up as best I could and put a smile on my face, much like the ones I use when presenting seminars. Within five minutes I had increased the range of motion in my neck and my back felt better. My brain got the message. Send positive messages to your brain.

Your mind is not the only part of you that needs to remain positive. It can be just as important to be positive from the neck down.

Positive Posturing

Although it is very important to have positive messages coming from the brain, it is equally important to have positive messages coming from the body. When you are tired, depressed, or discouraged, how do you sit? Most people slump, perhaps with the head hanging down. This posture does not allow adequate blood supply to the brain. No wonder you feel bad; your brain is starved for oxygen!

The next time you're feeling down, sit up. Throw your shoulders back, chin up, put a smile on your lips. Send a message to the brain that says, "Hey, up there! We're okay. How about you?"

Assets	Liabilities
● Listening to what you say to yourself (be positive!)	● Accepting a limiting thought as truth
● Paying attention to the advice of your left hemisphere, then questioning it	● Reading or listening to negative communication the last thirty minutes at night or the first thirty minutes in the morning
● Being especially positive to yourself when you know your "guard dog" (left hemisphere) is off	
● Notifying your body that you're doing fine: shoulders back; chin up; smile!	

Nurture your mind with great thoughts
for you will never go any higher than you think.

BENJAMIN DISRAELI

*People are always neglecting something they can do
in trying to do something they can't do.*

ED HOWE

KILLING THE MESSAGE, NOT THE MESSENGER

y now I hope you are convinced that words and thoughts are powerful. They have physical ramifications. There are two methods of handling the negatives. The first program is designed to help you make deposits right smack in the middle of your day when your left hemisphere is turned on and supposedly guarding you. This help may be temporary, yet very necessary to function through all the stress. This is your Public Attitude Plan, and it allows you to get rid of the negative and maintain a healthy attitude. It enables you to kill the message, not the messenger.

PUBLIC ATTITUDE PLAN

You want to be positive, yet the world is basically negative. To remain positive, you must realize who the enemy is. The enemy is not a person; it is what the person says or does. In order to defeat this enemy, you must recognize it, realize its power over you, and counterattack with powerful weapons of your own. If this is starting to sound like war, you're on the right track.

STEP ONE: IDENTIFY THE NEGATIVES

The first step is to identify the negative words and thoughts that come your way. Some of the more common negative ideas that come from other people include

"Can't."

"It won't work."

"I'll try."

"It's not my job."

"I just work here."

"We've never done it that way before."

"I don't have the time."

"You're kidding."

"Who do you think I am?"

"Paaaleeeeze!"

"No way."

"Are you crazy?"

"It's not in the budget."

"I'll call you when I'm interested."

Common negative thoughts that we tend to give to ourselves include

"I'm tired."

"I'm stressed."

"I have too much to do."

"No one appreciates me."

"I'm fat."

"I'm too old."

"I'm not good enough."

"I don't have enough experience."

"No one ever listens to me."

"I'm ugly."

"I don't know how."

"It's not my fault."

Sometimes the enemy comes in the form of negative gestures: a frown, a furrowed brow, a shrug of the shoulders, rolled eyes, perhaps a sneer. These usually come from a submissive communicator who later may not even claim ownership of the message — you know, the "I didn't say anything" mentality. Don't kid yourself. The message was clear and just as defeating as if the negative words had been spoken.

Start today and notice the negative words and phrases around you. Write them down, and at the end of the day I'll bet you have at least a full page. If not, tune in more closely tomorrow. If you're around people, the negative messages are there.

Where do these negative words and phrases come from? Let's start close to home. In fact, start with yourself. Even if you consider yourself a positive person, you probably give yourself a fair, or not so fair, share of negatives. Next, look around you. Your family and friends can be pretty

> The enemy is not a person; it is what the person says or does.

negative, too. Just because they love you doesn't mean they're always positive. People tend to take out their frustrations on the ones they love the most. Co-workers can complain about traffic, weather, the customers, the boss, too much work, too little work, money, family, politics — even you, if you're out of earshot. Employees and managers are not exempt from complaining either. And then there are the media. Tune into any station that offers news and hear a torrent of negatives.

When I first began my university studies, I joined the forensic team, which allowed me to travel to many colleges in the United States to participate in public speaking contests. One time I entered the broadcasting portion of the contest. I wanted to be different and fill my ten minutes with good, wholesome news. The week preceding the event, though, I was unable to find ten minutes of good news on the Associated Press wire.

Some veterans from the Vietnam War have told me that one of the difficulties they experienced was not knowing who was the enemy. It might have been a villager or even a child. The first step in this program is identifying the enemy: the negative words, phrases, gestures, and thoughts that influence your most precious commodity — your mind.

STEP TWO: EXPLODE THE NEGATIVE

These negatives fill you with worry and guilt. We become burdened and weighed down by all the garbage we carry around. Get rid of it!

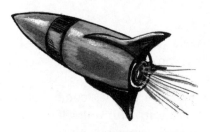

Think of step two in terms of a military defense. If the enemy sends an aircraft to inflict negative thoughts on you, shoot it down with an anti-aircraft missile. Your armed forces in this war on negatives are your right and left hemispheres. For your missile, come up with one word — any word that you find suitable. To fire your missile, repeat the word twice with emphasis. My missile is "Cancel! Cancel!" This personal missile tells my brain to shoot down the negative message. It's my way of telling myself not to store the negative message in my memory or let it harm my attitude.

The word you choose for your missile is entirely up to you. Others have chosen missiles such as

"Stop Stop"

"Delete Delete"

"Go Go"

"No No"

"Erase Erase"

"Reconsider Reconsider"

"Dump Dump"

"Garbage Garbage"

"Light Light"

"Help Help"

I even had one client whose missile was "Pizza! Pizza!" The word you choose doesn't matter; what's important is to choose only one word and to say it twice. The left hemisphere of the brain, which controls language and logic, cannot argue with just one word. Your missile will have a better chance of intercepting the incoming enemy if there is no interference from the left hemisphere.

Take a moment to create your missile. You can change it later, but stop right now and at least come up with one word that you will say twice. On a piece of paper write down, "My missile is _____ _____."

Every time negatives try to enter your mind, use your missile. For instance, if one of your goals is to fight fatigue, and you hear yourself say, "I'm tired," immediately say your missile — for instance, "Cancel Cancel." If you are excited about a project and a co-worker rolls her eyes, silently recite your missile.

Saying the missile out loud is more powerful than just thinking it, but use your common sense. If you say your missile out loud, some people may be offended, others may think you've lost your marbles. I do encourage you, however, to inform close friends and associates that you are identifying negatives and destroying them. This can help you remember your task, and it just may encourage them to be more positive around you so their words don't get blasted!

STEP THREE: USE POWERWORDS

Science tells us that once a void has been created, something will fill it. After you have used your missile to de-stroy the negative word or thought, fill the void with a positive one. These are called PowerWords because they are indeed powerful. A PowerWord is one positive action-filled word that you repeat over and over. Let's say you need to persuade your boss to allocate funds for new machinery. You feel, however, that she won't listen to you. There, you've identified the problem: your negative thought. Immediately blast it with your missile and then replace it with a PowerWord such as "Influence! Influence! Influence! . . ." Repeat the PowerWord until the positive feeling takes hold of you. You may need to use it again in a few minutes; that's okay. Old negative habits, like putting yourself down, are difficult to break.

Let's look at some other examples. If you have a presentation you need to make in the next five minutes but you're tired, your PowerWord might be "Energize! Energize! Energize! . . ." If you're angry at an individual, your PowerWord could be "Calm. Calm. Calm. . . ." When you need to persuade someone to buy into your idea, the PowerWord can be "Convince! Convince! Convince! . . ." Say it as many times as necessary to make the negative thought go away.

Think about challenging situations that come up during your day. Plan some PowerWords to use so you'll have them ready when you need them. This trick really works, as long as you remember to use it.

With practice, you'll find that using the Public Attitude Plan takes only seconds. It's an effective, time-saving way to make the first deposit of your Four Deposits for Balance: Set your attitude and your altitude.

Assets	Liabilities
• Being alert to your environment (identify what gets you down, then explode it!) • Using your missile every time you perceive something negative • Telling those close to you what your missile is and what it does • Replacing negative thoughts and words with PowerWords	• Repeating negative words or ideas to yourself • Investing your precious time in worry and guilt, which will wipe out your balance

*What you dislike in another
take care to correct in yourself.*

THOMAS SPRAT

*The future belongs to those who believe
in the beauty of their dreams.*

ELEANOR ROOSEVELT

DIRECTING YOUR
SUCCESS

 or long-lasting posi-
tive effects, you need
to plan your attitude
the same way you plan
your day. This takes only fifteen or twenty minutes a day.
Before you convince yourself that you don't have twenty
minutes, remember what being positive can do for you —
bottom line, it can change your life.

In the previous chapter we discussed a quick fix, the Public Attitude Plan. Now it's time for a more permanent solution, the Private Attitude Plan. You can use this one either the first thing in the morning or the last thing in the evening. The best time is when your left hemisphere is turned off so that it cannot argue with you. Thus, you can direct your success without interference.

PRIVATE ATTITUDE PLAN

STEP ONE: MAKE AFFIRMATIONS

Affirmations are positive sentences. They are not necessarily true when you say them; rather, they are what you

want to be true in the near future. Think of them as "positive lies." Affirmations are what you want to be, not what you fear to be. There are specific rules to follow when making affirmations.

Use the first person. The first word in the affirmation should be "I." After all, you control only yourself. If you want someone to listen to you, it does no good to affirm that "Joe listens to me," because you are not affirming or programming to Joe's right hemisphere. Instead, think of what you can do differently with Joe. For instance, "I notice when Joe looks at me." When you start concentrating on this, you'll probably find that Joe looks at you more than you realized. Remember, the first word of an affirmation is "I."

Use the present tense. Present tense happens here and now. The brain responds to urgency. Do not say, "I will speak up"; rather, "I speak up." In other words, don't put it in the future; say it as though it were happening right now.

Make them positive. It doesn't make much sense to go to the trouble of identifying a need only to be negative about it again. By being "positive" I mean literally no use of negative words. For instance, there should be no use of the word "not" or any form of it. Instead of "I don't forget," say, "I remember." Also avoid using words that have a negative connotation to you. Say, "I am reducing my size" instead of "I am losing weight," because both "lose" and "weight" may be negative for you.

Following these three rules of affirmations, take ninety seconds and jot down five affirmations for yourself. These can be job related or personal. If within ninety seconds you write down three to five affirmations, it demonstrates that you know what you want.

STEP TWO: VISUALIZE

Saying a positive sentence (affirmation) is powerful, but adding the other senses to it is amazing. Take each affirmation and, in your mind, attach your own movie to go with it. In this movie, you get to be the director. You get to decide the cast, props, scenery, and dialogue. For instance, if your affirmation is "I am calm when I talk to Beth," see yourself in a room with her. Visualize every detail of the room: color, size, lighting, objects, furniture,  and so on. Hear her voice. Feel yourself shaking her hand. Smell the fragrances. Mentally place a snack in the room and taste the food.

The more senses you include in your "movie," the more you will convince the right hemisphere that you are really experiencing being calm with Beth. When the meeting actually occurs, your brain will think, "Hey! This is nothing. I can be calm with Beth again." This is truly directing your success.

One of my clients, a successful salesperson, wanted to be the divisional sales manager for his company. He wanted to prove his value as a manager and had gone as far as writing and posting his goal. When he began directing his success through mind movies, he started having fun. He visualized the new title on his business card, his special parking space, his increased bonus checks. He mentally solved opportunities with customers and encouraged his peers to reach for the stars.

While he was directing all this in his head, those around him started noticing a change in his performance. He started thinking and acting like a divisional sales manager. When he actually got the promotion fourteen months later, he said the reality was a little different from his mind movie, but he felt prepared to handle the new responsibilities. He had already started on the next movie he planned to direct: "Vice President of Sales and Marketing"!

STEP THREE: ATTACH AN EMOTION

We have all experienced positive emotions. While you are daydreaming (visualizing) in step two, attach a positive

emotion. Remember the last time you felt happy, elated, proud, satisfied, contented, or loved. Then simply attach the memory to the daydream.

This is not just parroting, "Be happy, don't worry"; it is directing your attention to the positive aspects of your life. Focus on what you can do instead of worrying about what you cannot do. Worry is nothing more than a negative private plan. When you worry, part of your mind feels as though the dreaded events were actually occurring. Choose to be positive! Practice in your mind so that you will be prepared for whatever life sends your way.

When you are really down in the dumps, it can be difficult to use the Private Plan because of the habit of worry. During these times, take physical action. Exercise changes the chemistry of the brain and lets us get beyond the wall of depression and doubt. Remember the three M's: Move and Mind Movie!

I strongly encourage you to spend twenty minutes each day to get yourself centered on the positive. Decide to be a thermostat, not a thermometer. Don't just react to the events of the day; choose a plan. If you're a skeptic, try it for ten consecutive days. If you want to change your life, change your attitude. If you want to be successful, direct your success.

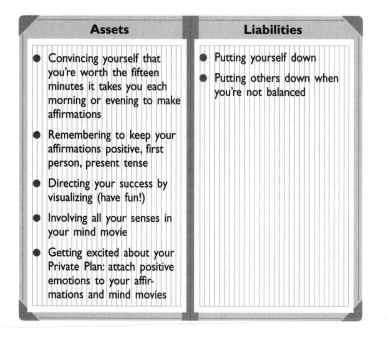

Assets	Liabilities
• Convincing yourself that you're worth the fifteen minutes it takes you each morning or evening to make affirmations	• Putting yourself down
• Remembering to keep your affirmations positive, first person, present tense	• Putting others down when you're not balanced
• Directing your success by visualizing (have fun!)	
• Involving all your senses in your mind movie	
• Getting excited about your Private Plan: attach positive emotions to your affirmations and mind movies	

During the time of the darkest night,
act as if the morning has already come.

THE TALMUD

SECOND
DEPOSIT

LISTEN MORE
THAN YOU
TALK

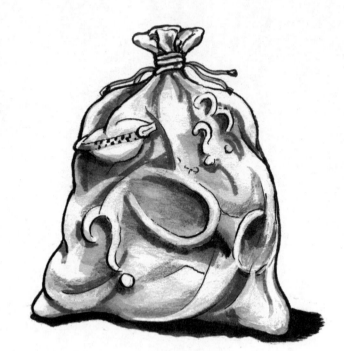

SECOND DEPOSIT:
LISTEN MORE THAN
YOU TALK

A good listener is not only popular everywhere,
but after a while he knows something.

WILSON MIZNER

CONDITIONS
FOR LISTENING

he process of communication can be quite simple: while one person is talking, the other person listens; then they reverse roles. Unfortunately, this seldom happens. Many times we are so busy composing our response that we do not truly listen to what the person is saying to us. We spend more time talking and planning our talk than we do listening.

Make the second deposit of Four Deposits for Balance: Listen more than you talk. It sounds simple. It makes sense. So what conditions keep us from listening?

We are poor listeners when

- someone says something significant and we go off in our thoughts to find a solution or compose a response;

- we don't like or respect the person who is talking;

- we don't agree with the information or opinion;

- outside distractions, such as noise or commotion, compete for our focus;

- internal distractions, like pain or hunger, command our attention; or

- we consider the information boring or repetitive, which shuts down the left hemisphere.

We are sometimes led to believe that listening is a passive skill. How many times were we told as a child to "sit still and listen"? But true listening is an active skill that can be harder than talking. A study reported by Madelyn Burley-Allen (*Listening: The Forgotten Skill*) revealed that a manager spends 40 percent of his time listening, only 35 percent talking. These statistics indicate that we should all strive to improve our listening skills.

I asked many successful CEOs and presidents of large companies how important they considered listening. Without exception they ranked listening as the most important of all skills to develop and utilize. One bank president told me he got to his position by listening. In his early years, he said, his colleagues thought him an introvert and therefore no competition for promotion. While others were writing him off as just a good old boy, he was actively listening his way to the top.

Another client of mine, an executive with Coca-Cola, was promoted to run a multi-billion-dollar business in Atlanta. His goal — which he accomplished — was to spend the first three months listening. He learned so much he is still listening to this day.

Most of these managers earned degrees that supposedly prepared them in their areas of expertise. Certainly all have acquired, in their life experience, skills that enable them to be more effective. Yet 40 percent of a manager's paycheck is earned simply by listening. I wonder how many of these managers have ever studied the art of listening.

●●●●●●●●●●●●●●●

DECIDING WHEN TO LISTEN

Most people need to improve their listening skills, yet there are times when listening is not appropriate. One should be able to identify these times immediately and postpone listening. It may not be appropriate to listen, for example, when

- you are already engaged in listening to another person,

- you're working on an urgent deadline, or

- you're hurrying through the plant to handle an immediate crisis.

When you need to postpone listening, quickly make eye contact, tell the person precisely when you'll get back to her, make a note of it, and continue with your current activity. However — and this is all-important — when you postpone listening, be sure to carry through with your promise. You must get back to her at the appointed time, even if it is to tell her you need to reschedule until after the emergency. It's better to postpone listening, and be able to listen well later, than to half-listen at an inappropriate time. Remember, the first time you fail to follow through, know that you have made a huge withdrawal in your account with that person.

Sometimes you just need to put a person on hold for a minute before you listen. Quickly establish eye contact, then raise your finger to signal "just a minute." Keeping your hand in this upraised position, look away and quickly finish your task. Most people will patiently wait; as long as your hand is up they know you haven't forgotten them. Drop the arm and they'll either leave or interrupt you again. Even young children have learned this rule. If you don't understand why this works, raise your arm in this position and see how long it takes before your arm tires. Pain is your reminder that you have someone on hold.

Gadgets can also help postpone listening. Place a bulletin board or a space for post-it notes on your door so potential interrupters can jot down their message rather than giving it to you verbally. Respond promptly to each written message. Using voice mail and e-mail can also postpone listening as long as these tools are not misused or avoided.

Don't postpone listening just for convenience. If you do it too often to too many people, you'll soon get the reputation for being too busy to listen. Postpone infrequently and with care.

When you do decide to listen, there's no turning back. Don't start listening and then decide to postpone. This results in a withdrawal from your account. Some people have good intentions but give the impression they're not really listening; the problem could be that they're having trouble focusing.

COMMON DON'TS WHEN LISTENING

- Don't answer the phone.
- Don't continue your work at your desk (or anywhere else).
- Don't think you can to two things at one time.
- Don't look out your door or window.

> *Don't postpone listening just for convenience — you'll get a reputation for being too busy to listen.*

Three Levels of Listening

Level One: Listening to Focus. Includes eye contact, head nods, pauses.

Level Two: Listening to Understand. Includes verbal input to verify meaning.

Level Three: Listening Beyond the Words. Includes reading body language and tone of voice.

Let's examine the first level in detail so you can determine how well you focus.

LISTENING TO FOCUS

There are specific things you can do as a listener that will enhance your ability to stay focused. These include making eye contact, pausing, and nodding your head. Each is important in focusing your attention on the speaker and convincing the speaker that she has been listened to.

Eye Contact

Since 55 percent of information we receive is visual, it's easy to understand why maintaining eye contact as a listener is very important in staying focused. There is a saying: "Where the eyes wander, the mind will follow." If we allow ourselves to be distracted visually while listening, we'll soon recognize a gap in that listening ability.

"Where the eyes wander, the mind will follow."

There are several reasons to make eye contact:

- It lets you observe the speaker, which gives you additional information.

- It's good manners and a kind thing to do.

- Most people who do not receive eye contact will repeat themselves, which wastes your time and theirs.

- It sets the expectation that if you give your attention, you will get their attention when it's your time to talk.

Back in the early '80s when I was interviewing with a television news director for a consultant position on the news staff, I had an interesting listening experience. The news director, whom I'll call Bob, was sitting with his heels on his desk and his fingers laced behind his head. Bob would ask me a question and turn his eyes and head to his right while I gave my answer.

At this particular time in my life I wanted this opportunity to work with the television station. More immediately, I wanted Bob to look at me when I gave him my answers. I felt I wasn't being listening to.

After talking to the side of his face for two answers, I decided I would change my tactics. After he asked his third question and looked to his right, I leaned forward and turned my head in the same direction to see what was capturing his attention. To my astonishment, there were three televisions, each set to a different network station. He was watching television instead of focusing on my answers!

I leaned back in my chair and relaxed, realizing how insignificant this interview was for this man. I also put a smile on my face. Noticing the pause, he quickly looked back my way. Once I had his eye, I answered his question with a newfound sense of humor. His feet came off the desk and he leaned forward with new interest. We had an excellent working relationship for four years and are friends to this day.

Many people find they have more difficulty getting eye contact than giving it. Perhaps they go to talk to the boss, who says she has time but continues to fiddle with folders and papers on her desk. Sometimes you just need to let the person know that eye contact is expected by

- pausing until she makes eye contact;

- quietly calling her name; or

- asking for her attention: "Mary, I feel there might be something else on your mind right now. Do you want to reschedule this meeting?"

Some people, especially introverts, have difficulty giving eye contact. Although most are better at it when listening than when speaking, there are many reasons why an individual doesn't look at the speaker, including

- shyness,
- habit, and
- feeling negative about the topic.

At other times it's the environment that makes it difficult to give eye contact. It can be as simple as the distance between the speaker and the listener. Most conversations take place at a distance of three to five feet. Many people have difficulty maintaining eye contact if the conversation occurs over a distance of more than five feet or less than three feet.

This is especially true in a business setting. Conversations that occur between people more than five feet apart can be sustained, but the answers will be brief and to the point. Let's say you're at a customer's office. You walk into the reception room; only one other person is there, and it happens to be someone that you know and haven't seen for awhile. If he's more than five feet away from you, the conversation will be short with brief answers. You'll both probably resort to reading a magazine, or one of you will get up and move closer to continue the conversation.

Interpersonal Space

0–1.5 feet	Intimate Zone
1.5–3 feet	Friendly Zone
3–5 feet	Conversational Zone
5–10 feet	Unfamiliar Zone
>10 feet	Formal Zone

It's basically your right as a human being to receive eye contact when you're speaking, and it is your obligation to give it when you are the listener. Of course, there are exceptions. For example, when you're driving a car, I, as well as the insurance companies of America, prefer and advise that you keep your eyes on the road. Rather than following the letter of the law in this instance, follow the intent.

Giving and receiving eye contact is a critical element for effective communication.

Pauses

A pause is a one- to three-second nonverbalization while maintaining eye contact. Any pause shorter than one
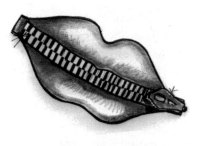 second is merely a breath. Pauses longer than three seconds can make the communicative partner feel uncomfortable; with others, you may lose your turn to talk. It's very important to maintain eye contact when you pause; otherwise people will simply
think that you've finished talking or that you have nothing to say.

In listening to focus, using pauses gives you many advantages:

- You will be perceived as a good listener.

- You will gain time to plan what to say, because you can think much faster (500 words per minute) than you speak (150 wpm).

- Your conversations will be more serious and less excitable.

- You can get additional information out of people after they have partially answered.

There are many situations when a pause can be useful:

- Pause after your communicator partner has finished speaking, instead of jumping right in, which makes it obvious to everyone that you were dying to get in your two cents' worth.

- Pause after you've been asked a serious or complicated question. Those few seconds can make the difference between success and failure.

- Pause when you feel an argument coming on. By slowing down the rate of exchange, it may keep you from saying something you might regret later.

- When you are interviewing someone, pause before you ask another question to get additional, perhaps more spontaneous, information from them.

- Pause when you are conversing with children. Give them time to comment and initiate conversation.

Slow down just a bit; the world is moving fast enough. Place some pauses in your communication and make them work for you. Get comfortable with some silence. You'll be amazed at what you hear.

Get comfortable with some silence. You'll be amazed at what you hear.

Neutral Comments

A final component of listening to focus includes neutral comments. Basically, these are head nods and little sounds you make in your throat. These vocal and nonvocal comments help to keep the other person talking because she feels listened to. Let's talk about head nods first.

When you are really intent on listening, unconsciously you will occasionally shift your head posture. You may tilt your head to the left or the right or move it slowly up and down. The key word here is slowly. Please realize that this slow head motion does not mean you agree with what the person is saying; it simply means that you are agreeing to listen to what he is saying. Now if your head nods speed up rapidly and you start to look like one of those dog statues in the back window of a car, you've changed the message completely. Now you're saying, in effect, "Shut up so I can talk."

One of the big differences between looking at someone and staring at him is the nod. When you maintain eye

I was coaching two clients: Mary, a manager, and Joe, the department director. Mary complained that Joe never really listened to her. Joe stated with great sincerity that he thought he did. I videotaped one of their conversations in which Mary was expressing her concerns. Although Joe could later recall her words quite accurately, Mary felt rejected and not listened to. Then we watched the tape. Joe had listened without moving his head. He looked bored and unsympathetic. When he learned the importance of head movement and practiced using it, Mary and other managers reported that Joe was now easier to talk to.

contact but keep your head still — that is, staring — you're saying, whether you mean to or not, "I'm getting tired of listening to you and I'm taking over." If you really do want someone to shut up, simply stop moving your head. If you really do want to listen, simply keep shifting your head posture. People will talk longer and tell you more.

The other type of neutral comments is the little sounds that you make with your throat. You do this naturally, especially when you are listening on the telephone. Some examples of neutral comments include

"All right."	"Is that right!"
"Okay."	"Gee."
"Oh."	"Go on."
"Oh, that's interesting!"	"Hmm."
"Huh!"	"Then what?"
"No kidding!"	"I see."
"Really."	"Sure."
"Uh huh."	"Um."
"Yeah."	"Oo."

It's very important to keep these comments neutral. There's a tremendous difference between saying "uh huh" with no inflection and saying it as though excited or in agreement. The first will keep the person talking; the second is interpreted as a judgment and will usually stop the flow of information.

The purpose of a neutral comment is to encourage the speaker to keep speaking. It is usually quite evident over the telephone when neutral comments are not made. The person on the other end may be going into great detail about a certain matter. If you do not grunt or make any of these noises, within a few minutes you will probably be asked, "Are you still there?" Of course, neutral comments do not ensure that you are listening; it merely gives the impression that you are.

Sometimes, in an effort to get a person to quit talking, people make the error of using a rapid stream of neutral comments. Instead of getting the individual to stop talking, however, this tells him that he needs to hurry up, which usually causes him to ramble and repeat himself nervously. If you want the other person to stop talking, don't use neutral comments.

Assets	Liabilities
• Choosing to listen	• Attempting to accomplish a mundane task while you listen
• Immediately postponing the conversation when you cannot listen	• Staying behind your desk for sensitive conversations
• Giving eye contact	• Agreeing to listen but failing to silence your own thoughts
• Requesting eye contact from others	
• Pausing to listen better	
• Moving your head slowly or changing head positions while listening	
• Making neutral sounds occasionally to let the person know you're listening	

We keep our power
by protecting the power of others.

THOMAS MOORE

*The only way to entertain some folks
is to listen to them.*

FRANK McKINNEY HUBBARD

HELPING PEOPLE OPEN UP

s young children, we were all taught the importance of waiting our turn. In making deposits with people, we need to remember this primary lesson. Instead of responding as soon as an idea pops into your head, continue to listen. Silence yourself and make the second deposit in Four Deposits for Balance: Listen more than you talk. You'll find it a great way to encourage people to communicate.

Refraining from being the talker is key to this second level of listening. In listening to understand, you must listen completely to what people say and compare it to what you think they mean. The more they talk, or the more they open up, the easier this task should be. Sometimes people give very brief answers or are unwilling to speak. When this occurs, you should be ready to use a probe. In general terms, a probe is an instrument used to explore; for you as a communicator, the probe is a question or comment that allows or encourages your partner to talk.

There's an old saying: "He who asks the question controls the conversation." There's a lot of truth to this. If you're still trying to control people, I strongly encourage you to abandon that goal. Strive instead to control what people talk about.

Not all questions are created equally. Some questions will get people started talking, while others will end a conversation. It is important to realize the power of questions and to anticipate the type and length of response they will evoke. Let's take a closer look at the probes that get people to open up and communicate.

Karen went to the board meeting with her mind made up. She was convinced that buying the upgraded equipment was absolutely necessary. Ignoring the fact that the industrial engineer was attending this meeting for some reason, Karen boldly stated her view as soon as the topic was opened for discussion. Then the IE took his turn — and she soon understood that, for half a million dollars less, the company could get the same results by reconstructing the existing equipment. This was definitely a time Karen would have benefited by asking before telling.

StartProbes

A StartProbe is a very open type of question that invites a flow of information. It usually requires a response of more than one word; thus, it gets the other person to start talking. StartProbes typically include questions that begin with these words:

how	what	when
where	who	why

You'll usually get the longest, most detailed answer in response to a "how" question. Perhaps it's because most of us don't like to admit that we don't know how to do something. A "what" question is also a very open question.

On the other hand, questions that begin with "who," "when," and "where" will generally get shorter responses, because they can often be answered with a single word. They sound more focused or targeted, and thus tend to intimidate people and make them defensive. If your goal is to be a listener by getting a person to open up, begin with "how" or "what."

The StartProbe that puts people most on the defensive is the "why" question. "Why" is negative because people internalize it. With some, it makes the hair stand up on the back of their necks, and they're ready for a fight. If you ask me why I did something, I immediately begin to defend myself, thinking that you are questioning my judgment, my ability, or my intention.

However, "why" is often a question for which you need an answer. The trick is to change the form in which you ask it. Here are two that work well:

"What are the reasons?"

"How come?"

When you ask, "What are the reasons?" you're going after the same information; you're simply bypassing the defensiveness. There's no need for the person to defend himself, his integrity, or his position. He can now talk about something outside himself; he can give you the reason. It's amazing how this simple change can reduce defensiveness.

I especially like the "How come?" substitution. Although this is less formal and somewhat agrammatical, it catches people off guard. Use it when a person who has some authority over you gives a negative response. She'll give her reasons, and you'll be the wiser for it.

GENERAL TIPS FOR STARTPROBES

To get the best results from StartProbes, some basic guidelines are helpful:

Ask only one question at a time. Sometimes people will destroy an excellent StartProbe by asking more than one at a time. When a person is asked multiple questions, he usually answers the last question he hears.

Former President Ronald Reagan, a great communicator, was an exception. He could handle even multiple questions. I remember a televised press conference in which an eager reporter asked a series of five questions, a process that took about three minutes. Ronald Reagan looked right at the reporter and said, "Yes. Yes. No. Yes. No. Next?" turning his attention to another reporter.

Most of us don't fall into the habit of asking five questions at a time; however, we often take the same question and keep revising it until we end up with a narrowly focused question: "What do you think of this idea? Do you think it will really work? I mean, I know we have to get approval, but I think the boss will give us an okay on it, don't you?" In this example, a StartProbe is reduced to a closed question, then further reduced to a leading question. When you are in the middle of a conversation, you may not ask a perfect question. That's okay; let the question stand. You'll get another opportunity to revise or refine it later.

Keep the questions positive. Questions should be free of any form of negation, such as the words

| not | don't | won't | shouldn't |
| couldn't | aren't | isn't | |

In the attitude section we discussed the effect negation has on the brain's decoding process. Negation requires a second and separate process. Therefore, when you ask a negative question or a question that has any form of "not" in it, you confuse the person who's about to answer it. For example, someone asks, "Don't you want to go?" Now, let's say you do want to go; is the correct answer yes or no? Most people will get a little confused and simply respond, "Sure, I want to go." However, if the question were made positive — "Do you want to go?" — people would have no difficulty because the question would be clear. Since the purpose of asking questions in the first place is to get the other person to start talking and to gather information, cut out the confusion by cutting out negation. Keep your questions positive.

Listen thoroughly to responses. Sometimes you may not like the answer you get; you still need to listen to it. You can hardly do worse than asking someone a question, then interrupting or demonstrating that you're not listening to the answer. If you find yourself getting into this habit, keep paper and pencil nearby. After you ask the question, zip your lip and listen. If something occurs to you in the middle of the person's response, don't interrupt; jot it down and keep listening.

Keep questions short. Long, complicated, or rambling questions can confuse or mislead the person being asked, making him feel stupid. This puts him on the defensive, and defensive people are lousy listeners. Keep your questions down to ten words or so.

Place qualifiers at the beginning of the question. Don't say, "What changes do you recommend, considering the budget?" Instead, say, "Considering the budget, what changes do you recommend?" As soon as the human brain hears the "what" or "how" word, it immediately knows that a question is coming and begins to compose its response. If the crucial part of the question comes at the end, the individual answering the question will probably have to recompose the answer to fit the qualifier. This is unnecessary work that can provoke frustration and defensiveness.

Opening up people allows you to be the listener and to learn more. Since everyone has something to say, as well as a basic human need to be listened to, using StartProbes can lead to major deposits in your people accounts.

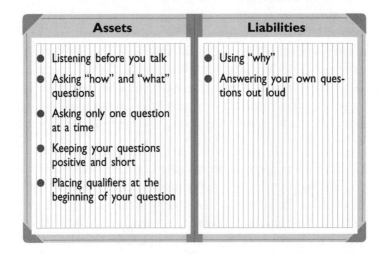

Assets	Liabilities
● Listening before you talk	● Using "why"
● Asking "how" and "what" questions	● Answering your own questions out loud
● Asking only one question at a time	
● Keeping your questions positive and short	
● Placing qualifiers at the beginning of your question	

Men are never so likely to settle a question rightly as when they discuss it freely.

Thomas B. Macaulay

*It takes two to speak the truth — one to speak
and one to hear.*

HENRY DAVID THOREAU

REACHING THE SILENT COMMUNICATOR

sking someone a question and not getting an answer can be very frustrating. It puts you off balance. When it happens, you need to be careful not to make a withdrawal from your people account. "Listen more than you talk" seems difficult to apply when the person isn't talking. In order to listen, you need to ask again, making sure you use a similar question.

When someone doesn't answer a question, most people will change the question. For instance, you ask your colleague, "What do you think about this idea?" She shrugs her shoulders. You come back with, "Well, I think it has merit, don't you?" This second question is a leading question, one that's not likely to get you an honest or spontaneous response. You might never find out how your colleague really feels about this idea.

You may ask the best "how" or "what" question imaginable and still be unable to break through to the silent communicator. People can have many reasons for not answering questions, including these:

- They don't know the answer.
- They don't want to reveal the answer.
- They don't understand the question.

What do you do when someone doesn't answer your question? First, you must decide whether your question is important to you. If it isn't, you should not have asked it in the first place. With practice, you'll learn to edit questions before they come out of your mouth. If the question is important, however, then work to get an answer.

It's important to recognize when your question has not been answered. Dead silence, of course, is one giveaway. But some people are adept at masking their nonanswers. They may respond with a question of their own or a funny comment, or try to get you off track in some other way. Simply ask yourself, "Did he answer my question?" If he did not, use a TripleProbe.

TRIPLEPROBES

A TripleProbe is a series of three similar StartProbes focused on getting you the information you need. TripleProbes are most successful framed as "how" and "what" questions:

1. "What do you think of this idea?"

2. "How do you feel about this proposal?"

3. "What are your thoughts on this?"

Your purpose in using a TripleProbe is to get an answer to a question you genuinely want an answer for. It's important not to be diverted from that purpose. Therefore, don't switch questions. Use three questions that are similar — that get at the same point in slightly different ways. In the above questions, this is done with synonyms: think/feel/thought, idea/proposal/this.

If the individual does not answer the question because he doesn't understand it, a second, similarly worded question will help clear it up. If he doesn't respond because he doesn't know the answer, then a slight rephrasing of the question can help. If he doesn't answer because he doesn't want to, seeing your persistence can induce him to answer regardless.

TripleProbes are not meant to intimidate, just to get information. Although a TripleProbe is a tool that you use to control behavior, if you use it correctly it won't make the person feel controlled but will allow him time to compose a response. A slight rewording is usually enough to accomplish this without making him feel defensive, as he would if he heard the exact same words again and again. Keep your voice calm and ask positive questions. Making polite, nonconfrontational, even offhanded comments between the questions can help:

Wanda: "How is the new program working for you?"

Chris: (shrugs shoulders)

Wanda: "How's it going since it was installed?"

Chris: "It's hard to tell."

Wanda (recognizing immediately that this is not an answer to her question, rewording it once again): "I know time will give us more information. What's your reaction to how it's doing so far?"

Chris: "Well, I think it's basically a good program except for . . ."

TripleProbes increase your chances of getting an appropriate answer to your question. To go further than three questions does not improve your odds. If within three similar questions the individual does not answer your question, it's time to use another communication tool — perhaps a StopProbe (which we will discuss in chapter 10) if he's gotten off the subject, or a different StartProbe to see if he has information in a different area that might be related to your original question.

This tool helps you control the conversation and get the information you need. It allows you to listen more than you talk. The key is practice; TripleProbes are more effective if they seem like natural conversation. When you anticipate that a person may be hesitant or defensive, don't plan just one question; plan a TripleProbe. Practice until you can roll them off your tongue without pausing to compose them in your mind.

Assets	Liabilities
• Making sure your question is worth asking	• Using TripleProbes to intimidate
• Quickly ascertaining whether the person has answered your question	• Changing the StartProbe to a leading question
• Using a TripleProbe when your question has not been answered	

If you would hit the mark, you must aim a little above it; every arrow that flies feels the attraction of the earth.

HENRY WADSWORTH LONGFELLOW

A gossip is one who talks to you about others;
a bore is one who talks to you about himself;
and a brilliant conversationalist is one
who talks to you about yourself.

LISA KIRK

GETTING PEOPLE TO KEEP TALKING

here are times when people in your life really need to talk. They aren't looking for a solution, they're looking for a listener — so you listen. Yet somehow, even though you think you're listening, they don't feel listened to; neither of you feels satisfied. There is, however, a way to overcome this frustration and encourage the other person to keep talking. Learn to give the gift of listening through BridgeProbes.

BRIDGEPROBES

The BridgeProbe is another way of using StartProbes that, in effect, hands control of the subject matter to the person you're listening to. This is the opposite effect from the TripleProbe, which keeps you in control.

Here's how a BridgeProbe works. After starting the conversation with a StartProbe, preferably with a "how"

or "what" query, use the speaker's response to bridge to the next question. You might start by asking what the person did last weekend. If she tells you she played golf, ask about her game. Do not change the subject; let her responses lead the way to

your next question. BridgeProbes keep the information flowing and show her that you are listening.

Like StartProbes, BridgeProbes work best with "how" and "what" questions, because people give longer responses to these. Let's take a look at an example of using BridgeProbe to keep the conversation flowing:

You (using StartProbe): "What can we do to improve productivity?"

Speaker: "I don't think we need gimmicks, we just need to listen to the workers."

You (using first BridgeProbe): "What do you think we could routinely do to listen to what the work force has to say to us?"

Speaker: "Well, first of all, we need to be on the floor, not stuck behind our desks doing redundant paperwork. We need to walk around and ask how things are going. We also need some scheduled meetings with everybody attending."

You (using second BridgeProbe): "When we stop and ask people on the floor, how can we make sure we're getting good information?"

This conversation can continue as long as you are willing and able to bridge and the speaker is willing to answer — and the more the speaker says, the more choice you have in steering the conversation. Here's the same dialogue using different BridgeProbes:

You (using StartProbe): "What can we do to improve productivity?"

Speaker: "I don't think we need gimmicks, we just need to listen to the workers."

You (using first BridgeProbe): "What do you consider gimmicks?"

Speaker: "Well, I don't go in for contests or something that's going to, you know, put the different departments in competition with each other and all that rigmarole. I think we just need to get down to basics."

You (using second BridgeProbe): "So what are some of the basics you think we need to begin with?"

Speaker: "Well, I think we need to have some meetings and listen to the people and take action on their concerns."

You (using third BridgeProbe): "That sounds like it has promise. How would you describe an effective meeting with the work force?"

Compare this with the first conversation. Although they start off the same, you have a choice of bridging either the gimmicks remark or listening to the workers. You can see that your choice at each juncture determines the rest of the conversation. Although you may eventually get to the same point, the route and the scenery can be quite different.

There are specific occasions when it is well worth your time to use BridgeProbes. Among them:

When you want to build confidence in people. Taking the time to listen and to comment on what a person says is an ego booster.

When you first meet an individual and you want to know as much as possible about her. For this reason, I find BridgeProbes very useful in interviews. Most people rehearse their presentation before coming to an interviews; when you use a BridgeProbe, you can get beyond the canned response and delve deeper into topics that interest you.

When relationships have been impaired. This is an effective way to let a defensive person express himself without feeling that you're controlling him.

The magic of BridgeProbes is that there's no set number of times that you use them. You can use a BridgeProbe three times or twenty-three times in succession, depending upon the topic, the individual, and the time available. BridgeProbes are great to use at work, at home, and in your social life. Practice bridging when you don't need to repair a relationship or when you're not making that initial contact. Remember, you're not really trying to get anywhere; you're just enjoying the journey.

Don't use BridgeProbes when you're in a hurry to get information or to get to a specific point. If you were traveling in a car and wanted to get somewhere quickly, you'd probably take the interstate. Using BridgeProbes is more

> A BridgeProbe can get you beyond the canned response and into topics that interest you.

like taking a country road; you'll get there eventually (and gather more information), but not as quickly.

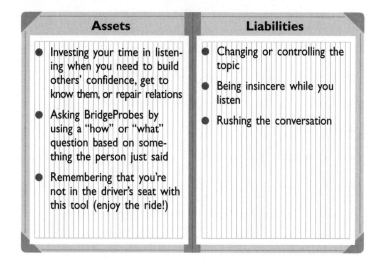

Assets	Liabilities
• Investing your time in listening when you need to build others' confidence, get to know them, or repair relations	• Changing or controlling the topic
• Asking BridgeProbes by using a "how" or "what" question based on something the person just said	• Being insincere while you listen
• Remembering that you're not in the driver's seat with this tool (enjoy the ride!)	• Rushing the conversation

What you are is God's gift to you, and what you do with what you are is your gift to God.

GEORGE FOSTER

You may be disappointed if you fail, but you are doomed if you don't try.

BEVERLY SILLS

GETTING PEOPLE TO STOP TALKING

lthough listening is very important, there comes a time when you need to stop the flow of communication. Unfortunately, most people don't verbalize this need, so their body language screams the message for them. They may stand up, move toward the door, or pull just about any move to send the hint that it's time for the conversation to be over. These subtle (sometimes not-so-subtle) hints can cause withdrawals in your people account. Instead of these acrobatic gestures, use a StopProbe.

StopProbes

You know that a StartProbe is a question that gets people started talking, so I'll bet you can figure out what a

StopProbe is. StopProbes are questions that require only a one- or two-word answer. They usually start with a verb, such as "is," "do," "can," "will," "are," or "have." Generally, they stop the flow of information, and so are most useful near the end of a conversation. Example: "Are you going to be able to finish this project on time?"

Here are some other examples of StopProbes:

"Is this correct?"

"Do you want delivery next week?"

"Can I make this change?"

"Will you call Wednesday?"

"Are you sure?"

"Have you checked the figures?"

Some StopProbes will give a forced choice or use a restricted "wh" question word at the beginning. Examples:

"Which do you prefer, A or B?"

"Do you want to go on Monday or Tuesday?"

"Where did he go?"

"Who called?"

"When is this due?"

StopProbes are useful tools; the problem is that they are often used incorrectly. Remember to use them at the end of a conversation rather than at the beginning. Sometimes a StopProbe is appropriate with the hesitant or distracted person; if he gets off track, it can get him refocused on the task. It's best not to use StopProbes with dominant extroverts; these probes are restrictive and make such people feel they are being controlled. On the other hand, StopProbes are especially beneficial with talkative communicators to reduce the amount of detail that you will receive.

Correct uses of StopProbes include

- checking for understanding,
- summarizing the point,
- nailing down a commitment,
- gathering specific data such as dates, times, and places, and
- requesting permission to speak.

When it comes to StopProbes, stop and think; use them, but don't abuse them. Let's take a look at another way to use these focused questions.

ParaProbes

Most people have a working vocabulary of about 1,500 words. Although our total vocabulary is much larger, these are the familiar words that we use in everyday life, especially in our career or business. Because of our different backgrounds and experiences, we all have different definitions for the same words. This is not surprising; open any dictionary and you'll see that most words have at least five definitions. Miscommunications can occur when one person is intending definition number one and the listener is hearing definition number three.

To avoid confusion over the message, use a ParaProbe. A ParaProbe, which is essentially a type of StopProbe, is a restatement in your own words of what you heard, often followed by a question:

Speaker: "I have three projects that need to be completed by the end of the week, and it's very important that we make the deadline."

You (using a ParaProbe): "So you need them completed by 4:00 p.m. Friday, right?"

It is important to use your own words. If you simply repeat the words the speaker used, you will only be demonstrating that you heard him, not that you understood him. In the above example, the speaker uses an ambiguous term: "end of the week." What is the end of the week? For most people, it's Friday, but is it Friday at 5:00 p.m., Friday noon, or Friday at 8:00 a.m.? To others, the end of the week would be anything after hump day, including Thursday. Some work on Saturday and consider that day the end of the week. To clear up the confusion, you used a ParaProbe, restating the key point in your own terms.

My family has hosted several foreign exchange students for an academic school year. Our Japanese student, Nana, showed me a picture of her younger brother. I said, "He's ornery looking." Nana, whose English was limited, opened her translation dictionary. Her face fell. I quickly looked to see what had caused her distress. All I could see were Japanese slashes that meant nothing to me. I grabbed my dictionary and thumbed to "ornery." The first definition was "devilish." I had just called her brother a devil! I was finally exonerated when I gave her the fourth definition: "spunky, mischievous." For the rest of her stay with us, I chose my words more carefully!

A ParaProbe is a good way of checking your deeper understanding of what the speaker is saying. It can uncover the ideas, concepts, and emotions behind the speaker's words. It's also an excellent way to improve your listening skills. If you know you're going to need to ParaProbe — restate in your own words

Restate in your own words what the individual has said.

what the individual has said — then it will make you listen a little better.

If you're dealing with someone who has a history of poor listening habits, you can ask her to use ParaProbes on you. After delivering your message, ask her to restate it to you: "Jill, in your own words, what did we just agree to do?" Listen carefully to check for understanding.

Using a ParaProbe can be a small investment of time that pays huge dividends in keeping your accounts balanced.

Assets	Liabilities
● Framing your StopProbe as a question that can be answered in one or two words	● Beginning a conversation with a StopProbe
● Using StopProbes mostly at the end of a conversation	● Using a StopProbe with a dominant communicator
● Using a ParaProbe to check understanding by restating in your own words what was said to you	● Using three or four StopProbes when one StartProbe would work better

●

Know how to ask. There is nothing more difficult for some people. Nor, for others, easier.

BALTASAR GRACIAN

*A man watches himself best
when others watch him, too.*

GEORGE SAVILE

READING
BODY TALK

In order to listen more than we speak, we need to listen beyond the words. Some people pride themselves on being good listeners, in part because they can repeat verbatim what the speaker says. Although there are many advantages to being a human tape recorder, this type of listening does not guarantee complete understanding. Many people insert meaning into their messages through gestures and expressions. Listening with our eyes to the body talk is part of the third level of listening: listening beyond the words.

Communicators who are focused more on people than on tasks have an easier time reading body talk for hidden messages. By becoming more aware of body language, we can all improve our skill at reading between the lines.

Let's say you're meeting a person for the very first time. You probably want to make a good impression. Fifty-five percent of that impression will be formed by your body language — visual information that includes how you walk, stand, and sit, how you occupy space, even what you wear. We spend most of our time thinking about what we are going to say, but I think this statistic reveals that we should spend more time thinking about how we are going to say it.

The two most important components of body language are change and speed. A quick change of posture can be significant. For example, if the person I'm addressing is sitting with his arms across his chest, it means little to me. If, however, he is sitting with an open posture and suddenly moves to a closed, arm-crossed posture, I take note. I know that something significant is going on in his mind, although I may not know exactly what.

> The two most important components of body language are change and speed.

Under stress, our body produces more adrenaline. In prehistoric times, the stress could have been the result of an attack by a large brown bear. A surge of adrenaline gave us the quick energy needed to stand and fight or to run away. In the business world today there are not too many big brown bears. However, your body reacts the same way when you experience stress sitting in a conference room, an office, or even your own home. When the mind detects stress, the adrenaline is sent out to the rescue. The result — in the office setting — is not fight or flight but perhaps a quick gesture. This is why speed and change are the signals to pay attention to when reading body language.

Body language is not an exact science; a given gesture has no specific meaning, and it is often changes of posture and their rapidity that carry significance. Keeping this in mind, I invite you to study the following general guidelines to how the body talks.

POSTURE

Posture can be defined as how one occupies space. Basically, the more space the individual occupies, the more relaxed he feels. A person leaning back in a chair with arms spread and legs crossed looks comfortable. People instinctively open up and talk more freely to this individual. (Of course, posture is always in context. Some body language may be too relaxed for the setting. If your boss catches you leaning way back in your chair with your feet on your desk, he may take exception.)

Several years ago I went to Washington, D.C., to work with a gubernatorial candidate. Our first meeting was to be at a political firm in Georgetown. I was well aware just how important the first impression would be. After introducing myself and giving my business card to the receptionist, I glanced at the empty waiting room to plan my posture. I was dismayed to find that the only furniture in the room was a human-eating couch — low, deep, and soft — that would swallow me and make it difficult to stand and meet my client. I didn't want to sit in it; neither did I want to be standing at attention, briefcase in hand, when he came around the corner. As I heard footsteps nearing the waiting room, I made a quick choice. I tossed my briefcase on the couch and perched myself on the arm. The first impression I made was that I was very sure of myself, relaxed, yet easily able to rise to my feet and offer a handshake.

If you are talking to a person who seems hesitant to communicate, examine your own posture. Sometimes simply opening up your posture, keeping your arms apart, especially your hands, and leaning back in your chair will increase the flow of communication. On the other hand, if someone is not taking you seriously or is talking too long, and you wish to send a message that says you are tired of being the listener, close your body posture. Sit straight; perhaps lean forward; bring your arms and hands together. Don't do it too quickly; you may startle the individual and stop him in midsentence.

If you're an introvert, you may be inclined to avoid confrontations and seek harmony. To give reprimands and corrections credibly, you may have to make a conscious effort to use appropriate body language. Close your posture; this will help send the signal that the conversation is serious and important.

When you enter a room, do you think about the space you will occupy? Some people gravitate to chairs and avoid couches; others are most at ease sitting at the corner of a table facing the door. Being relaxed — and sending that message — is a key to being an effective communicator. If you haven't thought of it before, stop now and consider what type of environment makes you the most comfortable.

In 1997, I was invited to a White House conference and reception that was held on the front lawn under a canopy. There were probably 200 people at this reception, and I knew no one. My first objective was to get a drink. It didn't really matter what was in the drink; it was just something to hold, to increase the space I was occupying, to make me look relaxed. Later, as the First Lady approached me to speak, I had freed myself of the drink so I could shake hands and gesture while speaking. Did all of this just happen? No, it was planned, carefully planned.

Often you will find yourself standing rather than sitting. The same basic rules apply: the more space you occupy, the more relaxed and confident you look. Bending the elbow has this effect. When standing, you can look more relaxed by holding something in your hand. Keep your feet shoulder width apart — which, of course, affords good balance — and even place one foot slightly in front of the other. A hand on the waist or a hand lightly resting in a pocket can be effective. Make sure your hand doesn't disappear into the pocket. Hands can do annoying things when this happens; they can jingle coins or keys or reappear with little lint balls on them when you go to shake a hand. Use your thumb to catch the seam of the pocket and place it there. Rest your hand; don't hang it.

Stand in front of a mirror. If your arms are straight down, you look very formal; hands clasped behind you looks like military parade rest. In neither case do you look relaxed. Adjust your posture; find a standing posture that's comfortable and looks relaxed.

Walking

Often people see you approaching before the conversation begins. They form an impression before you ever open your mouth. People can detect your mood and decide whether or not it's a good idea to approach you simply by watching your walk.

I was working with a plant manager who complained to me that his employees seemed afraid of him. As he approached his office building each morning, he could see that the workers who had arrived early were relaxed, talking with one another, and generally enjoying themselves before work. As soon as he entered the office, however, they all jumped to attention. No one spoke. Everyone immediately pretended to be on task. This really bothered my client. He wanted people to know that he was approachable. I arrived at the office one morning before the client so that I could witness his approach for myself. Attaché case in hand, he had a very quick pace with little or no arm movement. He kept his gaze straight ahead, not turning to visually acknowledge anyone he passed along the way. It was very obvious to me why he was not sending his intended message. I asked him to walk slower, turn his head from side to side, smile and give a social greeting. After the initial shock wore off, the workers adapted to his new routine.

An interesting study was done years ago in the State of New York. Videos of pedestrians were shown to inmates serving time for having mugged people. The videos were divided into groups of individuals who were similar in sex, height, and weight. Inmates were asked to judge which persons were "muggable." Their consistency was astonishing; they chose the same individuals. How did they make their decision? By the way the people walked.

Pedestrians whose upper body movement was not coordinated with leg movement looked awkward enough to mug. Individuals who walked slowly were also muggable; no one would miss them if they were detained. Another group of potential victims were those who directed their eyes from side to side. They looked nervous, and nervous people don't defend themselves well.

THREATENED PERSONAL SPACE

People act in predictable ways when they feel their space is being invaded. A change in eye contact is often the first sign. People will look toward an exit, a door, or a hallway, as if planning their escape. If you stand too close — closer than three feet, normally — the individual may find it hard to listen to you. Back up, give her more room, and see if the communication doesn't improve. Of course, you can also be too far away; this will get you brief responses. Three to five feet is best.

HEAD POSTURE

In most conversations the head is the focal point, because that's where eye contact is made. The way you hold your head sends a message. If you hold it straight, you communicate dominance. People will see you as all business, and you'll get short responses. This posture may be the most appropriate when you're correcting someone who has shown disrespect.

To increase the perception of willingness to listen, slightly tilt your head. Do you have a dog? Notice how your pet tilts his head when you talk to him. This is a dog's way of acknowledging that you're the leader of the pack. If you're engaged in a conversation with someone and you want him to share feelings and concerns, tilt your head slightly. It will soften your appearance, and it just may gain you the information you want.

MOUTH AND JAW POSTURES

You can often sense a person's true feelings by watching her mouth and jaw posture. Most people, when ready to listen, keep their jaw closed with the lips together but relaxed. An open mouth tells you the person is surprised; you may need to explain something to her.

Lips tightening can mean the listener is growing tense. If your listener's jaw begins moving from side to side, she is becoming agitated and less receptive to information. It may be time to stop talking and let her speak.

SMILES

Most people can tell the difference between a genuine and an artificial smile. With a genuine smile, the eyes are involved; facial muscles are retracted, which puts pressure on the tear ducts, making the eyes glisten. An artificial smile, however, does not involve the eyes. It looks as though the person were smiling only with his mouth.

Several years ago I had a client who was a contestant in the Miss USA pageant. As a member of the audience, I was allowed to see both the on- and off-camera activity. A certain actress was the picture of perfection when the cameras were on. Her smile looked genuine. However, as soon as the cameras were off, her smile fell like a lead ball from a fourteenth-floor window, and she would begin ranting about the poor conditions. It was obvious, to the audience on location, that her camera smile was indeed fake.

Another difference between artificial and genuine smiles is the speed of the movement. A genuine smile, although it may begin spontaneously, has a slow fade; it goes from a broad grin down to a more subtle smile. An artificial smile, on the other hand, can disappear as quickly as it begins. A genuine smile can mean that a person is receptive to having a conversation. An artificial smile, when identified, usually puts the other person in a state of distrust. Before you smile at the next person, make sure you genuinely feel like smiling. If not, you're probably not fooling anyone.

EYE BLINKS

People blink their eyes unconsciously and involuntarily to moisten the eyeball and to sweep away dust particles and foreign objects. Normally this happens in a regular, slow rhythm. Notice how someone's eyes may blink during a confrontation. Does the blinking become rapid? This is a sign of anxiety and usually means the person is not listening fully.

Conversely, a dead stare or less blinking than normal can also signal poor listening. The person may be deep in thought, perhaps about something you said earlier, but missing the current message.

H ollywood has long understood the message of eye blinks. Norma Jean was coached to blink her eyes frequently in front of the camera. Hollywood wanted to present Marilyn Monroe as a beautiful but dumb blonde. Obviously they thought dumb people didn't listen very well.

Of course, there can be other reasons behind rapid blinking — something caught behind a contact lens, for instance. Even if this is the case, you can bet the person is not able to listen well. If you notice a change in blink rate, one of the best things you can do is to pause and let the person recover.

EYE DILATION

A change in eye dilation can indicate the amount of interest a person has in what you are saying. Italian women who wished to appear more attractive to their suitors once applied drops of a natural cosmetic called belladonna ("fair lady") to their eyes. This caused their pupils to dilate, sending a tacit message that the lady was interested.

Scientists have documented that the eyes dilate when an individual's interest is piqued. A university study showed volunteers sets of two photographs of a person's face and asked them to choose which picture they were most attracted to. The only difference was that in one photo the eyes were dilated and in the other they were not. Most participants chose the pictures with the dilated eyes.

If you are in close-contact sales, such as jewelry, the degree of the customer's eye dilation may be important to you. In most conversations, however, you will probably not get close enough to notice. Nevertheless, when you go out to purchase that car of your dreams, wear sunglasses so the salesperson cannot clearly see your eyes. It could save you some money!

EYE CONTACT

An experienced communicator can glean a lot of information through eye contact. A sudden, upward eye roll is a distinctly negative comment, often interpreted as a put-down: "What a stupid idea." It's a signal of disapproval used more by introverts than extroverts. Eyes averted laterally signals evasiveness; it makes the individual's information seems less reliable or believable.

Here are some other key insights into eye motion:

Averting the eyes twenty degrees above the horizontal triggers the optic nerve, which facilitates visual recall. When someone is trying to visualize something, his eyes go automatically twenty degrees above horizontal. If you're the same height, his gaze may go to your hairline.

If a person's eyes go up twenty degrees and to his left, this can indicate that he is recalling visual information.

Eyes up twenty degrees and to the right tells that the individual is creating visual information. If the questions asked is "How can we solve this problem?" and the individual looks up and to his right, fine. He's creating a solution. If the question asked is "Where were you last Friday at 10:00 a.m.?" and his eyes look up and to the right, ask more questions. (Of course, there can be other reasons for eye movement. This observation is meant to be a guide to understanding, not a hard and fast rule.)

Eye contact can be a measure of how a person feels about herself. Eyes cast downward indicates low self-esteem. Don't talk to people who hold their heads down, because they're not listening to you — they are listening instead to all the negative messages already in their head.

When I go shopping in my community, I sometimes see a frustrated parent scolding a child in public. The child lowers her chin all the way to her chest, but the barrage continues. It's all I can do not to intervene. That child will grow up and one day go to work. When she makes a mistake and her manager tries to communicate with her, down will go the head.

When this happens to you, instead of talking to the top of the person's head, give her a reason to level it. Sometimes a pause will do the trick. Since she's momentarily incapable of listening, perhaps a nonthreatening question will get her talking. Suggest taking a walk as you talk. The activity can not only raise the head, it can raise the listening ability.

LOWER BODY GESTURES

A good way to put yourself under stress is to lie to another person. Your adrenaline surges, and though you may keep your upper body under control, your legs and feet may have ideas of their own. Watch carefully when you think someone is trying to be deceptive. Perhaps he's sitting with his right leg crossed over his left. If he suddenly shifts position so that his left leg is crossed over the right, his statement may not be entirely truthful.

The speed of this change in posture is important. A slow-motion change may mean simply that the person is physically uncomfortable and is perhaps shifting to ease a strained muscle. A sudden or spasmodic change, however, usually indicates that the person is uncomfortable with what he is saying.

TURN-TAKING BEHAVIOR

People do odd things when they are tired of listening and want to speak. It's important to be aware of these signals; otherwise, you're talking to a person who quite frankly is not listening. Look for the following signals:

- The person takes a noticeably deeper breath because she thinks she's going to get to talk. (Talking takes more oxygen than listening.)

- The person will open her mouth and quickly close it if you keep talking.

- The person will raise her index finger as if to pose a question or objection. This behavior is rooted in our early school days, when we waved our arms wildly to get the teacher to call upon us.

MANNERISMS

We all have physical mannerisms that we perform unconsciously. Some of us play with our jewelry or stroke our hair or beard; others pop pens or mangle paper clips. We do this more when we're feeling tired or negative. When he is about to tell me something I don't want to hear, my husband will pull a few hairs on the right side of his beard. Naturally, when I see this behavior I first dread the upcoming event, then prepare myself for it. That's the reason most of us hate the habits that our mates have. It's not that the habit is disgusting, it's that we see it when our spouse is in a negative mood.

Keeping an eye out for these mannerisms can help you know when to communicate and when to postpone. Let's say you are having a conversation with someone, and this person begins to crack his knuckles. Never mind the grating sound; be aware that this person could be feeling negative — perhaps about something you said, perhaps not. At any rate, in his negative mood, he's probably not listening well to you. It's not the best time for a serious, meaningful conversation.

To make the second deposit in the Four Deposits for Balance: listen more than you talk, and remember to listen with your eyes. You'll be amazed what you hear!

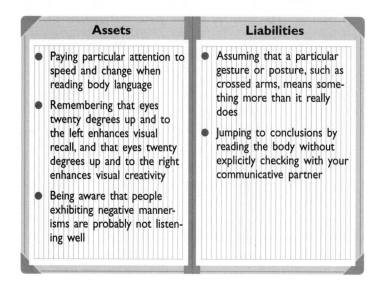

Assets	Liabilities
• Paying particular attention to speed and change when reading body language • Remembering that eyes twenty degrees up and to the left enhances visual recall, and that eyes twenty degrees up and to the right enhances visual creativity • Being aware that people exhibiting negative mannerisms are probably not listening well	• Assuming that a particular gesture or posture, such as crossed arms, means something more than it really does • Jumping to conclusions by reading the body without explicitly checking with your communicative partner

*People only see what they
are prepared to see.*

RALPH WALDO EMERSON

If God ever wanted my mouth any bigger,
he would have to move my ears.

BILLY KERSANDS

SECRETS OF
THE VOICE

n his 1972 book *Silent Messages,* Dr. Albert Mehrabian reported that 38 percent of the impression of a message is derived from the sound of the voice — more evidence that it's not what you say, but how you say it. I've had many clients who were dumbfounded by the way people have reacted to their messages: "What'd I say wrong?" They'd made a withdrawal on their people account without realizing it. What they need is to learn the secrets of the voice.

Think of the human voice as an instrument. This instrument comes in many shapes and sizes, producing a  wide variety of sounds. Some are high-pitched and harsh, like the screech of chalk on a blackboard; others are like the flute, making listeners feel lighthearted or excited; still others sound like the tuba, stirring deep emotions. There are three ways to vary the human voice: pitch (frequency), volume (loudness), and speaking rate. Other factors come into play: resonance, accent, and pronunciation. These are like the lyrics of a song, while the voice is the note played.

The equipment we use to produce our distinctive sounds are the diaphragm, lungs, pharynx, larynx, vocal cords, nose, and mouth. Each person has a distinct voice pattern, as unique as a finger print. A voice is so specific that even when you hear an attenuated voice over the telephone you can often tell immediately who's calling.

CHECKING YOUR PITCH

Some people like the sound of their own voice; others hate it; most never think about it. Many people speak at a pitch that is physically too high for them, especially women, while a few people speak at a pitch that is too low.

Do you ever think your voice is too high or too low? There's an easy way to determine whether you pitch is correct for your body. Sit back in your favorite chair, get comfortable, and close your eyes. Imagine that you've had a challenging day; now the day is over. Inhaling through your nose, take a deep breath; sigh out loud through your mouth and say "ah." Do this without expression; just softly breathe out a relaxed "ah." Try it a few times; listen to the pitch of your voice. This is the pitch that is physically best for you — the tone that your vocal chords make when you are relaxed.

Here's another test for pitch. Below is a series of closed questions or StopProbes. Read the questions silently one at a time, then answer out loud, saying either "uh huh" or "uh uh." When you give your answers, make sure you put no special emphasis or interpretation on the answer; just let the sound fall out of your mouth, not your nose.

"Is today Tuesday?"

"Is this the month of May?"

"Are the lights on?"

"Is it nighttime?"

"Are you reading a book?"

Each time you answer, listen for the pitch of the second syllable. This is the pitch that is best for you physically.

Now let's compare this relaxed pitch to your usual pitch. Below is another StopProbe, which I want you to answer with either "uh huh" or "uh uh." Immediately after that is a StartProbe for which you need to give a complete answer. Remember, read the questions silently. Give the answers out loud, through the mouth, and without added inflection.

"Is it summertime?"

"How would you describe your job?"

Now recall the difference in the pitch of your voice between the first and second responses. If it's almost the same, then you are using the conversational pitch that is best for you physically. If your answer to the second question was much higher pitched, then you may be speaking habitually in too high a pitch.

Here is a third check test for pitch. Hold up your index, middle, and ring finger so that they touch along the sides. Gently, without pressure, place the pad of the middle finger against your Adam's apple. Now start talking out loud.

You should feel a slight vibration on the pad of only the middle finger whenever you're using the pitch that is best for you physically. When you raise the pitch, you will notice a vibration on your index finger; if you lower the pitch, you'll feel the vibration on the pad of the ring finger. Unless you're speaking in a monotone, you should feel a little of both the higher and lower tones.

Now, pretend you're angry about something. With your finger still resting on your Adam's apple, scold some imaginary person. You'll probably notice that the vibration moved up toward the pad of the index finger.

Remember, this is a practice technique only. I don't expect you to walk around talking to your boss with the Boy Scout salute on your throat. On the other hand, if you find yourself being a listener on the telephone, place the three fingers on your throat to see if you're using the correct pitch on your neutral comments. If you are, the vibrations should be on the pad of just the middle finger.

CHECKING YOUR VOLUME

Volume boils down to hot air. It is determined by how much air is pushed through the larynx as the vocal cords vibrate. Talking louder means simply pushing more air through the pipes.

There are a couple of ways you can check your volume. One of the most accurate is to use a microphone hooked up to a tape recorder that has a meter to read input level. Watch the meter as you record your voice. Does it remain steady or does it rise and fall? Some plosive sounds, such as syllables with "p," will register high on the meter because more air pressure is needed to produce this sound.

Another way to check to see if you are having a volume burst is to place a single-layered paper tissue in front of your mouth. Gently drape it down from your nose. Speak a sentence — for example, "I am so ready to go home!" If you had a volume swell or a pressure increase on the "so," for instance, the tissue will move away from your face as you speak. If you can see the tissue move, know that others can hear the difference in your voice.

If people complain that you mumble, or if your volume is routinely too low, other things could be happening. Watch yourself speak in front of a mirror. How wide do you open your jaw? Except for short i and long e, most vowels require a jaw opening about one finger wide or more. Opening the jaw lets the sound come out. If your jaw looks closed or doesn't move much, people may have difficulty understanding you because you're muffling your voice.

WHAT PEOPLE READ INTO VOICE CHANGES

Many people, especially warm communicators, are very tuned in to your voice. When they hear increases in the pitch, volume, and speaking rate, they know the speaker is excited about something. Body language and word content will help determine whether the excitement is happiness or anger.

When people lower their pitch, volume, and rate, they are usually perceived as being serious — that they mean what they say. It's no wonder small children may take their father more seriously than their mother; his voice is deeper. People tend to prefer a deeper voice sustained over a longer period of time, one reason that male orators may be preferred over females. The deeper sound is more serious and more relaxing to hear.

> When people lower their pitch, volume, and rate, they are usually perceived as being serious.

The next time you are at a sporting event, notice the cheerleaders' voices. Both males and females raise the pitch and volume of their voice to excite you. When you have experienced a serious setback in your life, the person talking to you may use a lower pitch, volume, and rate to get you to calm down and think.

●●●●●●●●●●●●●●

READING BETWEEN THE LINES

I am amazed that when people learn a foreign language they often excitedly report that the interpretation of the message may depend upon the inflection of the voice. It is interesting that Americans are largely unconscious of how intricately dependent on inflection their own English language is.

Changing pitch, volume, and rate can definitely change meaning. I can take a five-word sentence and give it five different meanings by stressing different words. Read the sentence below out loud, saying the word in bold italics louder and higher.

"*I* want that brown dog." Hear the emphasis. I would be jealous if you got it, because I want the brown dog for myself.

"I *want* that brown dog." I would love to have the dog but for some reason am unable to obtain it.

"I want *that* brown dog." There are three or four brown mutts, and I want a particular one; perhaps the one in the corner, barking up the tree.

"I want that *brown* dog." There are several canines of different colors. It is the chocolate-brown dog that I want, not the black one.

"I want that brown *dog*." I am at a pet store. I see a brown dog, a brown cat, and maybe a brown duck. I want only the dog.

This is an elementary example of how inflection changes meaning. Most people instinctively discern these meanings without effort. Sometimes, however, the message that is being sent lies beneath the surface of the statement; it may have more to do with the attitude, emotions, needs, and preferences of the speaker than with the explicit information he is imparting. These subtle clues concern not so much the meaning as the speaker's attitude toward what he is saying.

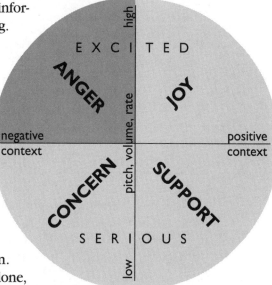

If you're a task-oriented communicator, you may have difficulty understanding or perceiving subtle differences in inflection. Although you are not alone, about 68 percent of the population understand these hidden messages in the voice. And when they communicate with you, they think you understand the code, too, and are less careful about word choice.

First, let's look at the big picture. In the voice inflection chart, the vertical axis represents pitch, volume, or speaking rate: higher than normal above the horizontal axis, lower than normal below. The horizontal axis represents the context of the speech: to the left, negative; to the right, positive.

VOICE LEVEL

The graph shows that if your pitch, volume, or rate is higher than normal, you sound excited; lower, you sound more serious. Now look at the upper left quadrant. When your pitch, volume, or rate goes up on the negative side of the graph, you will be perceived as angry. I call this the red zone — it's a dangerous place to be.

Many front-line managers will tell you, "You just need to yell at some people to get them to take you seriously." But I strongly believe that there's no purpose for talking in the red zone in a business setting. There's a better way: you can lower your pitch, volume, and rate. This gets the seriousness of your point across without bankrupting your people account. If you raise your voice when angry, you send a message that you're out of control. How in the world are you going to manage the behavior of others if you cannot manage your own?

When in doubt, speak low.

In a positive context (right side of graph), when your pitch, volume, or rate are high, you are more likely to be perceived as happy or joyful. Lower your voice, and you will sound friendly and supportive. It is sometimes appropriate to sound joyful — for example, you're a sales manager trying to motivate your sales force — and sometimes better to sound supportive, as when encouraging someone who has made a difficult but correct decision. Here's a good rule of thumb: When in doubt, speak low.

CONTEXT

What do we mean by context? Context is either neutral, negative, or positive, depending on (1) the message, (2) the situation, and (3) the personality type with whom you are communicating.

Message. Here's a negative message: "You're fired." A positive message might be "You won a million dollars." Can there be any doubt? In these examples, word content is patently negative or positive, so it really doesn't matter what you do with your voice — nobody will read between the lines. Want proof? Try telling someone, in a very soft voice, "You're fired." Or try to sound angry when you tell someone she's won a million dollars. Your negativity will not be catching. You may be frowning and growling; she'll be smiling and spending.

A clearly negative or positive message may not rely on inflection or tone of voice, but there are many neutral messages that do. For instance, "I want to talk with you" is basically a neutral message. Much of its meaning will be derived not only from the way it is said but from other aspects of its context: the situation in which it is spoken and the personality of the person speaking it. For example, a supervisor who raises one eyebrow and utters this phrase with a slight emphasis on the first four words will leave little doubt of her displeasure in the listener's mind.

Situation. Just as messages can be negative or positive, so can situations. I once called a business acquaintance on the telephone, one with whom I was on good terms and with whom I had communicated cordially before. I introduced myself, and was somewhat taken aback when she replied, in a clipped tone, "Yes?"

Because it was a telephone contact, I could not tell, of course, what was going on in her office. However, since I had no reason to think she was displeased with me, I concluded that she was probably involved in a negative situation at work and could not give me her full attention. We may not be able to control the situation our communicative partner is in, but we can certainly be sensitive to it.

Personality. Some people are negative by nature; others are positive. We've all known individuals who always expect the worst or who spend their lives complaining or demanding. We also know people who look for the best in every situation and handle whatever life throws at them. We cannot always choose with whom we communicate. Perhaps your customer is a negative person, or someone in your department or home has a negative slant on life. Be conscious of their voice inflections, as well as your own, because the true message may be read entirely between the lines.

LISTENING TO YOURSELF

Spend some time listening to your own voice. Some find it unnerving, even unpleasant, to hear themselves on tape, because they don't sound the way they're used to hearing themselves. You can't hear your voice correctly when you're speaking because what you hear comes partly through the bones of the skull. If it's a good recording, though, it's obvious that the taped voice is very much the way others hear us.

Record yourself

● reading a book out loud;

● conducting a telephone conversation (your end only); or

● participating in a face-to-face conversation (make sure the other person is game!).

Get used to the sound of your voice. If you don't like what you hear, tune it up. And remember, your voice is a precious instrument like no other. Treat it with care.

Yelling, smoking, drinking, and temperature changes just aren't healthy for your voice. Come to think of it, they're not so great for the rest of you, either.

Assets	Liabilities
• Being aware that people read between the lines when your voice changes in pitch, volume, or rate • Using one of the three tests to check your pitch usage • Remembering that your voice is a unique instrument and treating it with care	• Listening only to the words and ignoring how the words are spoken • Raising your pitch, volume, or rate in a negative context

Who you are speaks so loudly,
I can't hear what you're saying.

RALPH WALDO EMERSON

THIRD DEPOSIT

FIND A BETTER WAY TO SAY IT

THIRD DEPOSIT:
FIND A BETTER WAY
TO SAY IT

The time is always right
to do what is right.

Martin Luther King Jr.

RIGHT WORDS,
RIGHT TIME

et's assume you've done everything correctly up to this point. You know yourself and your tendencies. Your affirmations and PowerWords have paid off and you feel quite positive. In addition, you've done a marvelous job of listening. You've maintained eye contact, indicating your listening status by slowly nodding your head or making neutral statements. You have successfully read the body language and interpreted the voice inflections to get the complete message. Now what?

Now it's time for you to respond. Conversations are a give-and-take situation. You're never really finished with listening, but now it is your opportunity and "response-ability" to respond to the individual you have been listening to by saying the right words at the right time. That's what's behind the third deposit in your Four Deposits for Balance: Find a better way to say what's on your mind.

A common mistake that you can make at this point is to respond with a statement which demonstrates that you weren't listening but merely waiting to say something. It's important to avoid this mistake. The other person needs to be reassured that you were giving him your full attention. To do or indicate otherwise will result in a substantial withdrawal from your people account. Remember, talk is not cheap!

Here's a good way to get a reading on your "response-ability": read and answer the two questions in the following short quiz. Record your first impulse — that is, the answer that first strikes you as best. None of the answers is necessarily right or wrong in all circumstances, so don't worry, you won't be graded.

How Would You Respond?

How would you respond if a friend said to you, "This woman in my department got a promotion by brown-nosing the boss. That promotion should have been mine. I'm more qualified than she is. And besides, she doesn't even need the money."

A. "You probably haven't done your job as well as you think or you would have gotten the raise."

B. "It's hard to see someone get a promotion you were counting on, especially when you feel so qualified."

C. "Did you talk with your boss?"

D. "I think you should tell your boss how you feel."

E. "You did deserve the promotion. How unfair!"

How would you respond if an employee told you, "We're behind schedule and it's not my fault. I keep trying to get cooperation, but everyone is too busy with his own crisis. The bottom line is that the customer is going to be un-happy, and you know what that means."

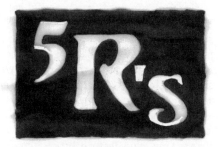

   A. "You should have told me about this last week."

   B. "Meeting deadlines can be very stressful."

   C. "How can we keep the customer happy?"

   D. "You need to calm down first."

   E. "I know this is not your fault."

Now that you've selected which response you would most likely give, let's take a look at five types of responses.

REBUKING RESPONSE

A rebuking response is a response that expresses criticism based on judgment; for instance, "You should have known better." If you're a parent, then you've probably found yourself using a rebuking response more often than you'd like. It's almost guaranteed to raise the emotional level of the conversation and, especially in a business setting, can easily be counterproductive.

Even when a rebuking response is warranted, it is often ineffective, especially in the work setting. A rebuked employee may spend an enormous amount of time justi-fying her behavior to herself and seeking out a listener who might agree with her. This can lead to blaming and a general lack of productivity. Rather than rebuke a per-son for her action or inaction, giving her information often works better because it allows her to rebuke herself.

RIGHT WORDS, RIGHT TIME

O ne spring weekend we took our boys, along with a couple of their friends, to a mountain retreat in the Cherokee National Forest in East Tennessee. Spring Creek Retreat is a beautiful getaway nestled in the mountains surrounded by a fifty-foot-wide creek with rapids and whitewater. On Friday evening, torrential rains began pouring down and continued through the night and early morning. That night, while sleeping with the window open, I was aware of not only the rain but the rising creek. Upon awakening, I went to the bay window and saw that the always lively creek had turned into a raging river. I went down to the living room to find my youngest son soaking wet. He had been playing in the creek. This seemed an appropriate time for a rebuking response. As one might expect, the child became defensive. I felt another rebuking response brewing, but changed my mind. Instead, I took him out to the deck, where we stood and watched the swift, muddy current roar down into a whirlpool where the boys' swimming hole had once been. Suddenly a huge log swept by like a motorboat. In another moment it was sucked down into the whirlpool and disappeared before our very eyes. Nothing I could have said would have had as powerful an effect. As they say, a picture is worth a thousand words.

In the two examples on the quiz, choices A were rebuking responses.

REFLECTING RESPONSE

A reflecting response is a nonjudgmental response that verbalizes the emotion of the message; for example, "I can tell you're upset." This allows you to be the emotional mirror and to reflect what the individual is experiencing. A reflecting response is invaluable when you don't want to get caught in the middle by having to agree or disagree. It lets you remain the listener and gather more information. By keeping you in the listener's role, the reflecting response also builds understanding and allows the speaker to find his own solution to the problem.

This type of response requires sensitivity and appropriate timing, of course. It is especially effective when used with other types of responses. Task-oriented communicators, however, may be uncomfortable with it and may have

A few years back, one of my business acquaintances was experiencing the traumatic breakup of her business partnership. I listened patiently to her lamentations but, never having had a partner, could not really identify with her. As a friend, I wanted to reassure her that she would enjoy being on her own, but I knew it was not the right time. So I used a reflecting response. Recognizing that much of her pain came from what she perceived as a loss of support, I said, "Feeling all alone can be frightening." My friend agreed. Then she said, "But I'm not really all alone." She began naming employees, business associates, clients, and suppliers who she felt would help her through the tough times. My reflecting remark allowed her to begin looking at the positive side, something I could not have accomplished with a more direct comment.

difficulty using it without sounding trite.

Avoid saying, "I understand." Although this is often intended as a reflecting response, it can actually increase defensiveness because the speaker may be quite certain that no one really understands him.

In the two examples on the quiz, choices B were reflecting responses.

REQUESTING RESPONSE

A requesting response is a response that simply asks for additional information, such as "What did you do?" This keeps the speaker talking. Be careful; if your timing is off, he'll think you're grilling him, especially if the requesting response is a StopProbe such as "Did you tell him no?" There's a world of difference between "What did you do?" and "Did you do such and such?" The first one is truly asking or requesting; the second is guiding or leading.

Requesting responses are especially valuable when you receive information from one party and then must go to another party and respond. It's dangerous to assume that you have complete or correct information. By using a requesting response and asking first, you can save yourself a lot of grief.

A manager had a reputation for high turnover in her department. Rumor had it that she just couldn't get along with people. One day a key employee reported that he was leaving. Jane listened attentively to his exit speech, then responded with a requesting response: "What part did I play in your decision to leave?" He told her that she had nothing to do with his decision; he simply had a better offer in another department. Jane asked him to put his reasons for leaving in writing to protect her reputation from further harm.

In the two examples on the quiz, choices C were requesting responses.

●●●●●●●●●●●●●●●●

RECOMMENDING RESPONSE

A recommending response is a response that offers advice, such as "Call right now and ask." Guess which group of people use the recommending response more than any others. That's right — managers. Managers feel compelled to answer questions and give advice. These are, certainly, among the roles of a manager. However, many are too quick to give recommending responses too early. Doing so increases the recipient's dependence on the speaker and hampers problem solving.

I advise managers to let their people bring problems to them, any problem in the world, as long as they also bring at least one possible solution to the problem. Whether this solution is the one that is actually used is beside the point; the idea is to teach people to think for themselves.

> People who find their own solution, or a least contribute to it, are more likely to embrace it.

Don't get me wrong — recommending responses are often necessary and effective. But before you give your next one, stop and ask yourself, "Do I have to provide the answer right now?" You may find it more helpful to use a requesting response, such as "What do you think?" or "What would you do if it were up to you?" or a reflecting response, such as "It sounds like this is holding you back." This gives the other person the opportunity and time to explore the problem further and perhaps solve it. People who find their own solution, or a least contribute to it, are more likely to embrace it.

In the two examples on the quiz, choices D were recommending responses.

RELATING RESPONSE

Agreeing with the speaker, as in "I know just how you feel, and you're absolutely right," can make the speaker feel understood. Anyone who has a complaint, whether she's an employee, a friend, or a family member, wants to know

---

No sooner had Joe been promoted to sales manager than he found himself in an uncomfortable situation. The company announced a new benefit package, and sales personnel complained to him that the reduced benefits would impose hardship on everyone. Joe agreed with them, and he told them so. This not only put him on record as opposed to upper management, it raised his people's expectation that he could get the company to reinstate the lost benefits. But Joe was not in a position to change the policy, and the benefits were not restored. Word soon spread that Joe was an ineffective leader, someone who just couldn't get things done. Joe then overreacted; the next time a new sales incentive was handed down, Joe publicly and wholeheartedly supported the company's position, even though he didn't agree with it. His sales force then began to see him as the enemy — and, worse, as indecisive and untrustworthy.

Joe could have avoided getting caught in the middle by not making relating responses in the first place. A good alternative would have been a reflecting response; rather than agreeing or disagreeing with the sales force, he could have said, "Changes in benefits can be very tough." He could then have taken their concerns to his immediate superior. The end result might still have been negative for the sales force, but they would have seen Joe as an advocate going to bat for them against tough odds.

that someone agrees with her. However, this kind of response — a relating response — can also reduce accountability. With everyone agreeing that life has been unfair, there's little incentive to find a solution. It's more fun to join the pity party than to work on self-improvement or increase productivity.

Warm, introverted communicators, driven by their need to relate to others, are most likely to use relating responses. This is a particular weakness of first-line supervisors who have worked their way up within the company and have to manage their former peers, many of whom are friends. They are no longer part of that group, nor are they part of upper management. They are continually caught between opposing viewpoints.

In the two examples on the quiz, choices E were relating responses.

Assets	Liabilities
● Listening before responding	● Using rebuking responses
● Using requesting responses to get more information and help the other person to find his own solutions	● Using relating responses in management
● Using reflecting responses to keep yourself out of the middle	
● Using recommending responses sparingly	

To get people to understand our point of view, we must first try to understand theirs.

SIDNEY KEYES

A problem well stated
is a problem half solved.

CHARLES F. KETTERING

INFORMATION, NOT OPINION

When you're trying to communicate information to another person, whether or not she receives it depends largely on how you present it. Information bound up with your attitude or assumptions is opinion; your listener may or may not be able to discern what is vital in the communication — the facts. For clear communication, you need to present information unpolluted by what you think about it.

STATEMENTS OF OPINION

In a normal thought process, you first gather information through your senses — you read, see, hear, feel, or otherwise experience it. For example, Sue enters the conference room at 8:45 for a meeting that started at 8:30. The general manager nods at her and gives her a smile. Sue yawns. As soon as your brain receives this information, you begin to try to make sense of it. You connect it with other data you have and arrive at some assumptions. For example, you remember that yesterday you heard Sue talking about a date she was looking forward to that evening.

Once you've assumed that she kept her date, you draw a quick conclusion — that she's tired because she was out late having fun. Your mind then proceeds to an opinion: Sue needs to be more responsible and take her job more seriously. But you may be wrong. There may be other, more favorable facts about Sue that you don't know, and expressing an opinion based on incomplete information could gain you a fast faceload of egg:

Person A: "Boy, I thought Sue was going to nod off for sure during the staff meeting."

You: "Yeah, she couldn't stop yawning. She needs to be more responsible and take her job more seriously."

Person A: "Oh, really? Well, she was up until three this morning finishing the report the general manager gave her yesterday at quitting time. I think she's being very responsible!"

We all go through this process of collecting information, making assumptions, and forming an opinion. It's only natural. However, unless you're asked for an opinion, always strive to convey pure information. Think back to the original information, then state the information rather than your opinion. You'd be a lot better off if the conversation went something like this:

Person A: "Boy, I thought Sue was going to nod off during the staff meeting."

You: "She seemed pretty tired. I understand she went out on a date last night."

Person A: "Actually, she didn't. As I was leaving for the day, I heard the boss ask her to finish his report for him. She stayed here till three working on it."

By keeping your opinion to yourself, you avoid misjudging the person in public, and you end up with more information than before, which can help you make management decisions.

Opinions are fairly easy to distinguish from real information. Here are some characteristics and limitations of opinions:

Opinions are nonmeasurable. If you say, "It will do a good job," how do you measure "good"?

Opinions are based on assumptions that can turn out to be false. It's usually best not to assume anything until you've gathered enough information.

Opinions are sometimes disguised as labels: "She is a Republican," "He's a Yankee." When you broadly categorize an individual, you appear to be implying that no further information need be given.

Opinions are often snap judgments. As with labeling (above), one tipoff to an opinionated statement is any form of the word "is" followed by an adjective: Becky *is happy.* Robert *was defensive.* They *were surprised.* The situation *is hopeless.*

Idioms are often entertaining, but they're not the best tool for clear communication. A client of mine in a top position at a manufacturing plant had a habit of using colorful idioms when he talked. One of his favorites was "Don't pee on my leg and tell me it's raining!" I often had to ask him what a particular idiom meant; his explanation seldom matched my interpretation. This one meant, "Don't accidentally pass on rumors."

Opinions often contain idioms, colloquial expressions that everyone supposedly understands but that can mean different things to different people: "A rolling stone gathers no moss." People sometimes use idioms when they aren't clear on the facts.

> When someone asks for your opinion, by all means give it; otherwise, give information.

An unsolicited opinion usually has a negative effect on people. Those who disagree tend to get defensive and will either argue with you or clam up. Either way, communication breaks down. Stop and ask yourself, "Is this what I want?" If it is not, give information that is not mixed with personal opinion. When someone asks for your opinion, by all means give it; otherwise, give information.

STATEMENTS OF INFORMATION

When you give information without opinions, it's almost as though your listener were there to witness the event for herself. This can be a tremendous benefit when communicating to upper management, who usually see the big picture but not the day-to-day details. Let's take a look at the characteristics of informative statements:

The information is verifiable — dates, numbers, names, and so forth. We usually have this information but fail to deliver it by not being specific. Instead of telling who, we may use a pronoun such as "he" or "they." Instead of a specific amount, we may say "more," "a lot," or "substantial." Rather than a specific date, we may generalize: "last week," "next month," or "some time ago." It takes more planning to speak informatively than in generalities, but it's time well spent. You'll get fewer questions and, in the long run, save time.

Informative statements are descriptions rather than labels. For instance, instead of saying, "John is late," you can say, "John arrived at the meeting fifteen minutes after it began." What's the difference? Well, perhaps John had an errand to run that pertained to the meeting and arrived, in fact, not late but exactly when he expected to. You may be the only person at the meeting who considers John late.

Informative statements focus on information, not on people. This forestalls people's tendency to assign blame and cuts defensiveness and aspersions on the character of others. Instead of an opinion statement, such as "Stella is lazy," use the informative version: "It takes Stella four hours longer than her co-workers to complete the same tasks." This lets the listener come to his own conclusion and keeps you out of trouble. It also increases others' respect for you; they'll consider you a fair player.

Informative statements are more likely to lead to agreement. It's easy for someone to have a different opinion, more challenging to have different information. Speaking informatively can lead to faster resolution of difficulties. This makes everyone look good.

Both information and opinion statements can be either positive or negative. For the negative opinion "She is rude," the corresponding negative information statement might be "Jane demanded an apology but suddenly left before one could be given." They are both negative, but the first

nformation vs. Opinion

Each of the opinion statements below has been changed to an information statement by adding verifiable data or describing what has happened.

Opinion:	Information:
This is great.	This project has increased customer calls by 20 percent.
They're not happy with us.	ABC Company complained that the parts keep breaking.
John was mad.	John quickly left the meeting.

The statements could be made even more informative by adding more information, such as when John left and which meeting he attended.

statement is more likely to get you into trouble. For the positive opinion "Rebecca is a good worker," the corresponding positive information statement could be "Rebecca has turned in her paperwork on time and correctly for the last three months." Although both statements are positive, the latter would help someone understand Rebecca's true value to the company.

Opinion, like information, can also be either true or false. People who hold strong opinions, however wrong, usually believe they're correct and may try to back them with erroneous information. You should understand that even if you're right, expressing your opinion is likely to make listeners defensive — but nothing will lose you their respect faster than giving them mistaken opinions or bad information.

STEERING CLEAR OF GOSSIP

Gossip is a wicked blend of information and opinion, usually offered by people who have no control over the situation. The more people, the more bold and exaggerated the gossip becomes, and the more likely to result in a mob mentality. Everyone hears gossip; responsible people don't spread it.

When someone is offering you information, ask yourself these questions:

● Is he giving me information based on his own observations?

● Is he in a position to change or control the situation?

● Is he willing to be named as the source?

If you answer no to at least two of these questions, it's most likely gossip. It's best not to scold or punish people who gossip. They'll do it anyway, and you'll just become part of the gossip. Instead, give them true, informative statements that will dilute the errors in the gossip. Be part of the solution, not the problem.

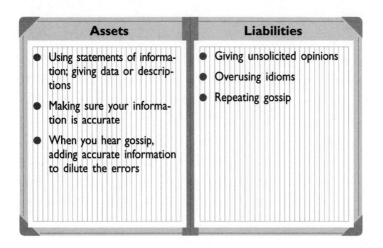

Assets	Liabilities
● Using statements of information; giving data or descriptions	● Giving unsolicited opinions
● Making sure your information is accurate	● Overusing idioms
● When you hear gossip, adding accurate information to dilute the errors	● Repeating gossip

The girl who can't dance says the band can't play.

Yiddish Proverb

He who praises everybody
praises nobody.

SAMUEL JOHNSON

CREDIBLE
COMPLIMENTS

 emember the last time
you got a compliment
that meant a lot to
you? Perhaps it came
from someone you respect. If you're like most people, you
put more stock in compliments from people in authority
than from others. However, the compliments that mean
the most to you are the ones that tell you exactly what
you did right, aren't they?

An informative compliment helps you to make the third deposit in your Four Deposits for Balance: Find a better way to say what's on your mind. It's important that the person believes that your compliment is sincere. Finding a better way to give it will make it believable.

Why do you give a compliment? Many of our clients give the following reasons:

- To motivate and encourage
- To give feedback
- To show appreciation

Continue to give compliments for these reasons, and for one other: to ensure that a particular behavior is repeated. This may seem like a rather selfish reason for giving a compliment, but if you've ever been in a leadership position, you'll quickly recognize its value.

Give a compliment to ensure that a particular behavior is repeated.

When someone does something correctly, obviously you want her to do it again. It doesn't have to be some extraordinary achievement; if she's simply doing what she needs to do, she deserves a compliment.

On the other hand, some people actually get embarrassed when a lot fuss and attention is turned their way, especially introverts. Does this mean they don't need to be complimented? I say no. All people need correctly given compliments.

HOW TO GIVE A COMPLIMENT

I'm sure you've received compliments that you just didn't believe. Maybe you were tired and having a bad-hair day, and someone told you, "You look great today." Or perhaps you limped to the end of a long, troublesome project and were told, "You did good work," when you felt your efforts were only so-so. Unfortunately, the lesson you may have learned from this compliment is that you didn't need to give 100 percent to gain that person's approval.

There are two steps in giving a correct compliment:

1. State exactly what the person has done that has gained your attention and approval. Instead of simply saying, "You did a good job," offer an informative compliment: "During the project, I noticed that you kept all members of the team informed. Thank you." This compliment sends him a strong message that keeping people informed is something you value. On the next project, you can bet that he will continue to keep people informed.

A sales manager and his entire staff were working on a proposal for a large contract. About three in the afternoon, his administrative assistant noticed a major error in the pricing and brought it to his attention. They worked until seven that evening completing the corrections. As they left, the manager said to his assistant, "Ellen, you did a great job. Thanks for your help." Understandably, Ellen went home with a glow.

Hoping to get the attention of her boss again, and a possible raise in salary — she needed the extra cash — Ellen spent the next three weeks working late. She thought what he appreciated was the extra time she put into her job. When he didn't show the expected appreciation, her enthusiasm wore off and she decided she was being taken advantage of.

The manager, too, grew discontented. He liked having the office to himself after 5:30 so he could get work done without distractions. He began to wonder why Ellen couldn't get her work done during normal work hours like everyone else. Was she becoming less productive?

This misunderstanding could have been avoided had the manager given an informative compliment weeks earlier: "Ellen, finding that error on the proposal helped save the contract. Your careful attention to detail made us all look good. Thank you." This would have told Ellen exactly what she did that was valued.

2. Let the person know how his actions helped you, the company, the team, or others. This makes the compliment more specific: "I noticed during the project that you kept the entire team informed. Although the information was not always positive, it helped each person feel like a valued member of the team. Thank you for that effort." When he receives this additional information, he has little choice but to accept and believe the compliment. This makes him even more likely to repeat the behavior.

A goal I assign my clients is to give one informative compliment to a different person each day. This practice is an excellent problem solver. Think of someone who gives you difficulty. Catch him doing something right. Plan a correctly given compliment, remembering to describe exactly what he did and how you or someone else benefited from it. Don't wait until he does something extraordinary; ordinary plus a correctly given compliment makes extraordinary. Get into the habit of recognizing what people do that is correct. Then just sit back and watch the results.

HOW TO RECEIVE A COMPLIMENT

A good way to ensure that you won't receive many compliments is to make people regret they gave you one. If someone compliments you on your good work and you reply, "Really? I'm surprised. I thought my work on this project wasn't as good as usual. I should've put more time

After a business organization meeting I noticed an interesting-looking purse sitting on a chair. I said, "I really like that purse. It has so many colors it would go with almost anything." The owner spoke up: "Oh, that old thing. I got that at Kmart for only four dollars." How do you think I felt? I was convinced I had very poor taste in accessories. That lesson taught me to be careful about complimenting people's attire.

and energy into it," how do you suppose that person feels? It will be a while before they risk looking stupid on your behalf again.

When you receive a compliment, all you need to do is stick your tongue between your teeth and say, "Thank you." You do not need to explain yourself or give reasons why you support or question the compliment. Simply say, "Thank you." Not only is that all that is expected of you, it is simply the right thing to say. Don't turn to mush and turn red, just say, "Thank you."

Assets	Liabilities
• Describing exactly what the person did and telling him how it helped you or the organization • Responding to a compliment with a simple "Thank you" • Catching a troublesome person doing something right and informatively complimenting her • Giving at least one informative compliment every day of your life	• Giving an insincere compliment • Declining to graciously receive a compliment

The man who desires to improve a human being must begin by appreciating him.

ROMANO GUARDINI

I praise loudly, I blame softly.

CATHERINE II, EMPRESS OF RUSSIA

CONSTRUCTIVE CONFRONTATIONS

hink how peaceful life would be if we never needed to correct anyone. Unfortunately, though, life is not like that. As friends, family members, and jobholders, we continually find ourselves having to set right the mistakes others make — and our own, when they are brought to our attention.

There are basically two kinds of mistakes that need to be corrected — those made knowingly and those made unknowingly. The latter are easier to correct. A person who gets something wrong because he is misinformed is less likely to take it personally if corrected. In fact, he may even be grateful for the instruction and consider it a learning experience. It's also easier for you, the person doing the correcting, to handle the situation diplomatically.

It's harder when you have to correct someone who is in error and aware of it. Depending on your personality type, you may react angrily at what you consider mischief, or you may avoid confrontation and try to compensate while the situation goes on or gets worse. Whatever your motives, it's easy to say the wrong thing and inflame the errant person's emotions.

It is important, in either case, to examine your motives. What you need to do is change the person's behavior, not berate or belittle the person himself. This is called "constructive correcting." If you are driven in part by a need to embarrass or dominate the individual, you are not correcting constructively, and the result may be not improvement

---

B illy's job in the plant was to mix the correct ingredients for the final product. One day, the second-shift supervisor altered the formula to meet the specific needs of one customer. He posted the required changes in the usual place, but Billy, perhaps out of habit, failed to make the adjustments. The result was lost time and an excess of waste product, which meant warehousing nightmares, scheduling difficulties, and lost income. When the mistake was discovered, the supervisor gave Billy a tongue lashing in front of everyone. Billy hung his head, ashamed of his mistake; still the verbal assault went on.

The question is this: was Billy corrected? The answer is no. He wasn't corrected, he was simply cornered with no place to go. He learned little from the incident but gained a new hatred for his supervisor. The workers who witnessed the dressing down were embarrassed; the supervisor went down in their estimation, as did the value of their jobs.

In hindsight, it's easy to see that Billy's mistake was partly the result of inadequate communication on the part of the supervisor. The supervisor could have anticipated that the break in routine would make mistakes more likely to happen. He not only failed to correct Billy, he failed to correct himself.

but resentment. To increase your chances of success, learn how to give informative corrections.

How to Give Corrections

To find out how the other person perceives the situation, lead off with a StartProbe — not so much to gather more information, because presumably you've been quite thorough, but to find out whether the individual is aware of her error. Starting with a question also lets the accused begin by explaining her actions. This may not excuse the error, but it does reduce defensiveness and ease communication.

Listen patiently to her response, whether it is short or long. To do otherwise is to signal that you really don't care what she knows or what she thinks about it. Even if your mind is made up, discipline yourself to listen to the answer. You may learn something you didn't know that will either change your mind or confirm your suspicions.

Next, describe the offense in an information statement rather than an opinion. This keeps the focus on the task, rather than on the person, and minimizes personal rejection and blaming. For example:

You (using StartProbe): "What's the reason the report is not finished?"

Employee: "I kept running into problems, and I just ran out of time. I need another week."

You (using informative correction): "We both agreed to this deadline so that we could ensure completion. Please remember that when we miss a deadline, we lose the trust of people who depend on us. I'll expect this report one week from today, and I'd like to see a progress report in two days. Now, let's discuss solutions to the problems you've encountered. . . ."

Notice that you lead off with an open question, a StartProbe, which begins with "what" or "how," to ensure that the answer will be as open as possible. You offer no comments or questions about the employee's problems, nor do you chastise her for mismanaging her time. You focus on the situation, not the person. You are careful to stay in control of the conversation; though you can't control what the other person says, you can lead the conversation where you want it to go.

Whatever type of communicator you are, you'll find that sticking to a plan makes giving corrections easier. Dominant communicators remain on task rather than going for the jugular. Warm communicators realize that a correction is not a personal attack but simply a tool to improve performance. Detail- and rule-oriented people learn not to get sidetracked on small issues but to focus on the correction needed.

Get to the point quickly. Warm communicators tend to talk about everything from weather to sports to food before getting to the point; they dread confrontation and want to lead up to it slowly, looking for a window of opportunity. It's misleading to carry on a social conversation and then turn around and correct someone. The individual knows that a correction is coming, so by getting right to the point you're actually helping the individual face the inevitable.

When correcting, get to the point quickly.

Don't correct an individual in front of others; this is very demeaning. It unnecessarily injures the person's self-esteem, makes other employees lose respect for you, and disrupts the team spirit that you need to make things run smoothly. Correcting in private, coming directly to the point, using information statements, and focusing on the problem rather than the person may not make you popular, but it will enhance your reputation for fairness and help keep your communication accounts balanced.

How to Receive a Correction

If you find yourself on the receiving end of a correction, you'll find that an informative correction is relatively easy to accept. Answer the StartProbe by giving information, not opinions. If you have different information, ask questions. For example, suppose you are being corrected for using accumulated comp time for a vacation day, and you believed this to be within policy:

HR manager (using a StartProbe): "How did you credit your day off last Friday?"

You (giving information, not opinion): "I had eight hours of comp time accumulated from my trips to New York, so I used it for recreational leave."

HR manager (giving informative correction): "Comp time can only be used in the same increments of time that it was collected in. Since you earned two hours on each trip to New York, it can be used in only two-hour increments. You're not allowed to take the eight hours all at once."

You: "Where is this explained in writing?"

HR manager: "It's in the employee manual, on page five under benefits, paragraph three. Here's a copy you can read. Let's go over it together."

By asking the question "Where is this explained . . ." instead of delivering an opinion such as "That's the craziest thing I've ever heard," you gather more information, keep your cool, and avoid putting the other person on the defensive. In the end, you may not like the correction, but you'll like the way you handled it.

Assets	Liabilities
● Asking for input before you correct	● Assuming you have all the information you need
● Stating the correction informatively	● Making the correction personal rather than task oriented
● Keeping on target	
● Correcting in private	
● When receiving a correction, asking for information you don't have	

The trouble with most of us
is that we would rather be ruined by praise
than saved by criticism.

Dr. Norman Vincent Peale

*An injury is much sooner forgotten
than an insult.*

PHILIP DORMER STANHOPE

WORDS THAT
SPELL TROUBLE

When you put someone on the defensive, he becomes a poor listener. The reason is simple. As a survival technique, he shuts down any further input to deal with the negative information he's already received. He may hear a word here, a phrase there, but in the end he may totally misconstrue your message and your intent. What he remembers of what you've said is likely to be incorrect.

The reason for a person's defensive behavior may be the personal baggage he brings into the conversation. Perhaps the situation reminds him of a previous bad experience, and the memory of what was said in the past gets in the way of what you are saying now. On the other hand, it could be something you are saying or doing now that sets off the defensiveness.

I once gave a client of mine, who was prone to cursing, a thesaurus as a gift. On the first page I wrote, "I swear you are too resourceful a man to keep using the same words over and over again." It was given with affection and received with good humor. By the way, his use of cursing drastically decreased.

Talking to a person who's on the defensive can make the problem worse. But you may not have the luxury of putting off the conversation, especially in a business situation. So how do you deal with defensiveness? You work to reduce it. You speak with information, not with opinions; you deal with the situation, not the person. And one further thing: you avoid using certain words that can cause a person to become more defensive. We call these "TroubleWords," because they cause more trouble than they are worth.

For each individual there is a particular set of Trouble-Words. Curse words, for instance; for many people they are not an issue, but others consider cursing immoral, impolite, or at least redundant. Still others deplore the speaker's apparent lack of self-control. People with deficient vocabularies often use them in place of more meaningful and informative words. It's usually best to avoid vulgarity.

There are many other words that can bring unexpected trouble; you may be surprised at their potential for mischief. Here are some of them:

You. This word internalizes information and shuts down listening ability. It is especially offensive when used at the beginning of a sentence, such as "You said . . ." or "You

did. . . ." Even if "you" did say it or do it, the individual reporting it may be taking it out of context or using a voice inflection that is sarcastic or demeaning. In a sentence with a negative connotation, it's like slapping "you" in the face or challenging "you" to a duel:

TroubleWords

you	but
always	never
no	try
should	must

"You said it would be ready."

"You don't understand."

"You're not listening to me."

"You think you're correct."

There are two solutions to omitting the "you" in the beginning of negative sentences.

Solution no. 1: Change the "you" into the "I":

"I understood it would be ready."

"I feel that I'm not being understood."

"I think I'm not being listened to."

"I think this is not correct."

Be careful about overusing "we." Though it may sound friendly and warm, unless both people involved are sharing the task and responsibility equally, it can cause hard feelings. Remember when your mother said to you, "We're going to get a shot today and we're not going to cry"?

Solution no. 2: Omit both "you" and "I":

"It was to have been ready."

"An understanding is needed here."

"Listening is needed here."

"It's important to be correct on this."

Task-oriented extroverts often overuse the "you" pronoun and can be very quick to point the finger at an individual. This may be so ingrained in your behavior that you're not even aware of it. The first step to changing any behavior is awareness. Start listening to yourself and to others. How often do you use the word "you"? When someone else is speaking and you feel the hair rise on the back of your neck, think back: did the individual just use the word "you" as the subject?

This kind of analytical listening is what Jayne Stephens, who worked with TLC, Talk Listen Communicate, LLC, and is now with Disney World, calls a "mental mike." Imagine that you can simply push a button, much as you would on a tape recorder, and replay what was just said. A mental mike is valuable in breaking habits and in determining exactly what you are reacting to. Use it to reduce the use of "you" and watch defensiveness decrease.

But. The word "but" negates previous comments and causes the listener to hear only the message after the "but." Although technically it is called a conjunction, this word doesn't really join anything; rather, it separates. If you go on a job interview and you hear, "I like your style, but you need more experience," are you going to be elated because the potential employer liked your style? Probably not. You're going to focus on her statement that you lack experience.

In our training group, it was agreed that whenever anyone used a TroubleWord, the others would throw a paper wad at the perpetrator. By the end of the session, one man was surrounded by a sea of crumpled yellow paper. His offense? He started most of his comments or responses with "but." He came back the next week and got through the meeting without uttering a single "but." He had told all of his direct reports to point a finger at him when he said the word. A few days of that treatment had cured him! Within a week or two, he started getting feedback from his people that he was becoming a better listener. It's amazing what one little word can do!

Solution: The solution for eliminating "but" is quite simple. Just omit the "but" and insert a pause or period in its place. Instead of saying, "You did a good job, but it cost too much," simply state, "You did a good job. It cost too much." By inserting a pause of one to three seconds, you allow the first information, the compliment, to enter the brain and be processed. The second issue, which is the cost, is then allowed to enter and be processed. It lets the individual hear the good news and then the corrective suggestion.

Always/never. All-inclusive or -exclusive words, such as "always," "never," "everyone," and "no one," reduce your believability and increase resistance to your information. Often we know exactly how many but, out of habit, substitute these words instead. If you say, "I always come early," your listener may remember a time four years ago when you arrived ten minutes after the meeting started. Not only will the listener dismiss your statement, she may begin to distrust other things you say.

    Solution: Replace all-inclusive and all-exclusive words with precise information. Instead of "I always come early," say, "I've been on time for the last nine meetings."

Should. This word is a control device that can produce guilt, a disabling emotion the effects of which are almost always negative. Upon being told, "You should call right now," the listener hears not only the suggestion, but a reprimand as well: "You should call right now. What an idiot you are for not thinking of this before. Do I have to tell you every step of the process?" This can lower self-esteem, which hinders listening and raises defensiveness.

    Solution: Instead of using the word "should," offer a suggestion or a question. Instead of "You should call right now," say, "You could call right now" or "How about if you call?" This may seem a minor change. Perhaps it is. But it's a minor change that can result in major improvements.

No. This word implies rejection, which increases defensiveness. It's often necessary to say no. Simply defuse it by going one step further: provide an explanation.

    Solution: Instead of saying, "No," explain: "No, because that will increase the time factor by two weeks, which is not acceptable from a profit standpoint."

Must. This word demands compliance: "You must make these changes today." Although dominant communicators may use this word, they do not like hearing it. Most people will work better and make the changes more readily if they understand the reason. Although it takes longer to explain why, in the long run it takes less time than it does to deal with a defensive person who does not wholeheartedly take action when the "must" word is used.

Solution: Instead of using "must," explain the importance of the action: "Making the change today will save the account."

Try. This word implies the possibility of failure without personal accountability. Many people use it with positive intent: "I'll try to get it done." In high achievers, this sort of statement can provoke defensiveness. They're not interested in whether you're going to try; they just want you to do it.

Solution: State what you can do. Instead of saying, "I'll try to get it done," say, "I'll initiate contact with all clients on this list. To those I cannot reach personally, I'll fax the data. Within three days I'll give you the results of the survey."

There are other words besides these eight that can spell trouble. People who like fast results may bristle at noncommittal words or phrases like "maybe," "kind of," and "sort of." Creative individuals may abhor any word that seems too restrictive, such as "exactly" or "precisely." Hesitant people may become defensive upon hearing "Just get it done!" or "You work out the details." Detail-oriented persons often dislike "bottom line," "general idea," or "ballpark estimate."

To maintain your communication account balance, make it a practice to know the type of individual you are talking to and curb your use of known Trouble Words. This can be an important first step in reducing defensiveness.

Assets	Liabilities
• Avoiding using TroubleWords by substituting specific information and terms that do not raise defensiveness • Thinking through the words that cause trouble for important people in your life, and finding other ways to communicate your message • Remembering that defensive people do not listen well	• Using words carelessly • Talking to someone who is defensive without making an effort to reduce his defensiveness

The bow too tensely strung is easily broken.

PUBLILIUS SYRUS

I have my faults
but being wrong ain't one of them.

HOW TO HANDLE
REJECTION

obody likes rejection. We like for people to agree with us, tell us we're right, and support us. However, nobody goes through life without experiencing rejection. Whatever the form this rejection takes, the important thing is how we handle it. And the key to handling rejection is this: don't get defensive, get information.

There are basically two types of rejection: direct and indirect. With direct rejection, you recognize immediately the other person's refusal to cooperate. Indirect rejection is more subtle; you may not recognize right away that you are being sandbagged, but the result is the same. Here's how to recognize and handle these different forms of rejection.

Direct Rejection

When you experience direct rejection, you know from the start that you are being told no, although the exact words you hear may vary. Direct rejection comes in three flavors: up-front rejection, venting, and antagonistic questioning.

Up-Front Rejection

In up-front rejection, what you hear is "No." Dominant communicators will probably stop at that. Others will try to explain further. The influential person will try to convince you that he's right. The hesitant individual will be

 anxious to reestablish harmony. The technical communicator will be convinced that you are interested in the minute details that led to her decision.

The technique for handling up-front rejection can be broken into five steps:

Step 1: Acknowledge it. Sometimes this can be verbalized by saying out loud, "Okay," or "I see." This does not mean that you agree; it simply confirms that you have heard and are not directly fighting the rejection. If there is any doubt of your meaning, clarify by adding an acknowledgment that you understand the objection: "Okay, I hear what you're saying." When they feel they must tell you no, most people go on the defensive and prepare to argue for their position; if you sound nonconfrontational from the start, it catches them off guard. The confrontation may make you feel defensive as well; starting off in a low key gives you time to cool off. You may say, "Okay. I'd like to revisit this after I've had some time to think." If your emotions are intact, proceed to step two.

Step 2: Use a StartProbe to get them talking. Remember, a person on the defensive doesn't listen well. This is not the time to explain your case or try to persuade him to change his mind. Instead, get him to give you the reasons why he told you no in the first place. Ask, "How come?" or "What are the reasons?"

Step 3: Use neutral comments to keep them talking. You may not like what the person says; you may think he is dead wrong. Keep this opinion to yourself. You asked the question; now you must listen completely. Nod your head; make neutral comments such as "Uh huh, I see." Remember, this doesn't mean you agree with the individual, simply that you agree to continue listening to him.

Step 4: Ask the question, "What else?" to find hidden objections. In my years of coaching people on how to handle up-front rejection, this is the step where it often breaks down. You may follow step one and say, "Okay." You may also remember to use a StartProbe, and if the answer doesn't knock your socks off, you may even manage to use neutral comments. The mistake you may make, however, is to assume that the first reason the individual gives you for rejecting your position is the real reason, and then to begin defending your position.

The truth is that your antagonist typically doesn't state the real reason up front. Often this is because he's not prepared to discuss it with you and just says the first thing that comes into his mind. If you get lured down this rabbit trail, you may never get to hear and respond to the real objection, and the individual remains unpersuaded.

Resist the impulse to begin defending your position too early. As soon as the individual begins to repeat himself or summarize his first point, ask, "What else?"

As the individual — under your coaxing — makes each point, jot it down on a piece of paper. Keep asking, "What else?" until he says "I guess that's about it," or words to that effect. There's something magical about the number three; most people give their real reason the third time they are asked the "What else?" question.

Resist the impulse to begin defending your position too early.

Step 5: Use a StopProbe to get a commitment or check for understanding. Say something like this: "So if I can A, B, and C, then you'll agree to my proposal, right?" What do you think the answer will be? Probably yes. At least then you know what you have to do to get a yes to your original proposal.

Here's how this five-step process might go in a typical case:

Employee: "What do you think of my proposal?"

Boss: "I appreciate the time you put into this, but it's not going to work."

Employee: "Okay, how come?"

Boss: "It's too time consuming. I can see this taking at least three months to complete."

Employee: "Okay, what else?"

Boss: "Well, there's the expense. Because of the time required and the equipment, it's going to be way over budget."

Employee: "I see, what else?"

Boss: "Well, I'm just not convinced it'll work. I'm not sure the theory is sound. There's absolutely no evidence that this will be successful."

Employee: "All right, what else?"

Boss: "Well, I have some other projects I'd like you to be a part of."

Employee: "Okay, what else?"

Boss: "Well, that pretty well covers it."

Employee (using a StopProbe to establish understanding and get a commitment): "So if I could reduce the time factor to, let's say, six weeks, which would also decrease the expense, and if I found ways to reduce equipment costs, supplied you with strong evidence that it would work, and still committed part of my time to other projects, then you would be agreeable, right?"

Boss: "Well, that's a lot, but yes. Yes, I would."

Employee: "I'd like an opportunity to get back with you. Can we meet next Tuesday?"

Now, there's no guarantee that the employee will be able to handle all four objections that the boss gave her. Perhaps she can; perhaps not. If she can, she has an opportunity to turn a no into a yes. If she is unable to meet the objections, she at least has an understanding as to how the boss thinks and can present future proposals that better address his concerns.

VENTING

Direct rejection in which emotion plays the dominant part should be considered venting. Reason takes a back seat to feelings as the individual shouts, complains, gestures wildly, and gets red in the face. Information content may be nil or misleading; the individual gets off topic, repeats himself, and generally makes little sense. This goes on for three to six minutes (if you listen, that is; interrupt, and it may go on for three to six hours!). How do you handle this?

You must decide instantly whether it's a good time to listen. If it is not — for instance, if it occurs in a group meeting — stop the individual and postpone the confrontation: "Joe, I can tell you have an important issue. I'd like you to stay after the meeting and talk with me about it. Right now, this committee needs to stick to the agenda. Our next topic is . . ."

As with ordinary up-front rejection, you can handle venting in a rational, step-by-step manner.

Step 1: Use neutral comments to keep him talking. It's very important to let the venting run its course. This will take only three to six minutes — if you don't interrupt. On the other hand, if you try to defend your position, jump in with a solution, or send a message of impatience through your body language, you'll only make the situation worse. You'll be making the person even more defensive, and defensive people are poor listeners. Instead, sit in a relaxed, open posture; lean back, cross your legs, keep your arms apart. Tilt your head or nod slowly to signal that you're listening. Interject comments such as "Uh huh, I see." Do not take issue with any idea you hear. This is not the time to correct.

Step 2: Use StopProbes to ensure that he is finished venting. Usually, by the time an individual hears himself repeat something for the second or third time, he will stop the venting on his own. When this occurs, simply use a StopProbe to ensure that he is finished, such as "Is there anything else you want to add?" If the individual resumes his tirade, then you know he was not finished venting in the first place. Go back to step one and allow him to wind down again on his own. Use another StopProbe. Then, if he's finished, proceed to step three.

Step 3: Use StartProbes to find solutions. At this point, with the venting apparently finished, you may feel it's a good time to offer a solution. This is a mistake. Just because the individual has stopped venting doesn't mean he's able to listen effectively or ready to consider your solution. You can come up with the best solution in the history of the world, and he will reject it, because he's still feeling very defensive. On the other hand, he may be ready to begin talking about a solution — and if he comes up with one, he's a lot more likely to accept it than yours.

Now, with the individual's defensiveness declining, is a good time to use a StartProbe. Asking him a question that begins with "how" or "what" lets him keep talking, but on a more constructive note. Example: "Okay, Bob, I have an idea of the problem. What do you think would be part of the solution?" Stay relaxed; as in the first step, listen patiently until he is finished. He may contend that there is no solution; in this case, use a TripleProbe, restating your question with slight variations to get him to respond directly. When he does venture a solution, don't reject it out of hand, even if it is ludicrous. Keep him talking and thinking. As his defensiveness goes down, the quality of his solutions will rise.

ANTAGONISTIC QUESTIONS

A third form that direct rejection may take is antagonistic questions. These are not serious requests for information; they are sarcasm, a form of venting, as in "Do you still think money grows on trees?" Your opponent may toss you an antagonistic question and continue venting, or he may pose one and stop, daring you to answer. What steps can you take in response?

Step 1: Whatever you do, don't answer the question. If you do, you lose. Even if you have the perfect answer, it will not be well received, because defensive people are poor listeners.

Step 2: If the person asks an antagonistic question and goes right on venting, not allowing you an opportunity to answer it, let it go. Do not interrupt to answer what was never intended to be a serious question. If you do, you only accelerate his defensiveness, and before long you're involved in a full-fledged argument. When you hear such a question embedded in venting, ignore it and use neutral comments to keep him talking.

Step 3: Even if the person asks you an antagonistic question and waits for you to reply, do not answer. Instead, use a StartProbe. Suppose he asks, "How stupid do you think I am?" and pauses, waiting for your response. How in the world do you answer that? You can't do it intelligently. Instead, toss a question back at him: "What makes you ask that?" This lets him keep talking, and you want him to talk, because he's still defensive and defensive people are lousy listeners.

It has often been said that there is no such thing as a stupid question. I don't agree. Most antagonistic questions are stupid questions. When you are asked a stupid question, don't make the mistake of giving a stupid answer. Throw the question back at the questioner.

As much as you dislike direct rejection, you can be sure that you will encounter it from time to time. As long as you have a plan to deal with it and follow that plan, you'll find it's not such a terrible thing. You can gain information from it. If you're a warm communicator, focus on the information, not the emotion; this will help you become more task oriented and less wary of confrontations. If you're already task oriented, stay focused on the task and become more sensitive to the person's emotions. If you're a dominant person and like to be in control, avoid catching the anger. If you're an unemotional communicator, don't think the other person a fool simply because he's momentarily lost control of his emotions.

When you are asked a stupid question, don't make the mistake of giving a stupid answer.

Above all, remember this: when you are confronted with direct rejection, your task as a communicator is to find the best way to get useful information out of the other person and find a solution that works for all involved.

INDIRECT REJECTION

I don't like to waste my time. I get especially annoyed if someone else tries to waste it for me. The third deposit, "Find a better way to say what's on your mind," really comes in handy when a person is wasting my time by delaying making a decision — in other words, by indirect rejection of my proposal.

Indirect rejection is the hidden "no." The sender of indirect rejection intends to tell you no. However, you'll probably hear everything except that word. You'll hear

- **Procrastination.** The individual may put you off by saying, "Let me think about that," or "I'll get back with you."

- **Rationalization.** The person gives you an excuse why something was not done. She may tell you, "I ran out of time," or "I have a few problems here; I'm going to need more time."

- **Meandering.** Instead of directly answering your question, the person changes the topic and starts talking about social events or any subject other than the one at hand.

- **Objection hopping.** You solve the problem, and he responds, "Yes, but . . . ," then gives you another excuse.

People who use indirect rejection are making withdrawals from their people account. They are letting people down easy because it's difficult for them to find the way to say what's on their mind. Let's discuss how to handle indirect rejection effectively in two steps.

Step 1: Use a StopProbe to stop the behavior. A closed-ended question will get the person focused on the topic at hand. In a situation where the person has rationalized and meandered off topic, the StopProbe used could be "Are you going to be ready by Friday?" If the person continues to procrastinate, rationalize, meander, or objection hop, ask the question again: "Are you going to be ready by Friday?" Notice that you're not using a TripleProbe, a series of similar StartProbes (open-ended questions). Instead, you ask the same closed-ended question again and again until you get an answer, because you want to nail down a commitment from the person.

Step 2: If you get the response you need, you're well on your way to reaching understanding. When you ask, "Are you going to be ready by Friday?" and the person answers, "Yes," go one step further, especially if you're dealing with a person who has a history of giving you indirect rejection. Ask him for a ParaProbe — that is, ask him to tell you what the agreement is: "Okay, Ned, tell me in your own words what you're going to do to accomplish this project by Friday."

If he says no to your StopProbe, treat it as up-front rejection. Open him up with a StartProbe to get him talking about the reasons: "What are the reasons it will not be ready Friday?" If he begins to give you indirect rejection again, state informatively that you cannot accept that reason. The exchange might sound like this:

Jo: "How is the project coming along?"

Ned: "A lot slower than I anticipated."

Jo: "How come?"

Ned (giving indirect rejection): "I've been up to my eyeballs in all kinds of projects. John has me working on something, too. In fact, I've been working such long hours that I haven't gotten on the golf course for three weeks! You know what that can do to your game. I bet if I went on the course today, I'd be slicing to the right the way I did before taking lessons. How's your game lately?"

> Don't let people waste your time giving you indirect rejection.

Jo (using a StopProbe): "Will you have the project completed by Friday?"

Ned: "Friday? This Friday? You've got to be kidding! Hey, have you heard who's coming to the plant this Friday?"

Jo: "Ned, the completion of this project was targeted for this Friday. Will you have it completed by then?"

Ned: "Well, I guess I could give it a try if I got some extra help."

Jo: "Tell me what you plan to do to make sure it's finished by Friday."

Obviously, this would not be the end of the conversation. Jo may need to listen carefully to the plan and then use another StopProbe, such as "So do I have your commitment to have the project completed by Friday?"

Handling indirect rejection requires task orientation. Your object is to stop the individual from straying. The simplest way to accomplish this is to keep coming back to the original question. Don't let people waste your time giving you indirect rejection.

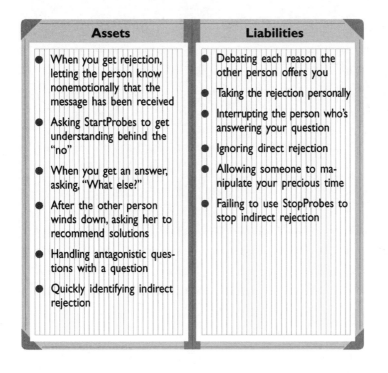

Assets	Liabilities
● When you get rejection, letting the person know nonemotionally that the message has been received	● Debating each reason the other person offers you
● Asking StartProbes to get understanding behind the "no"	● Taking the rejection personally
	● Interrupting the person who's answering your question
● When you get an answer, asking, "What else?"	● Ignoring direct rejection
● After the other person winds down, asking her to recommend solutions	● Allowing someone to manipulate your precious time
● Handling antagonistic questions with a question	● Failing to use StopProbes to stop indirect rejection
● Quickly identifying indirect rejection	

In the middle of difficulty lies opportunity.

ALBERT EINSTEIN

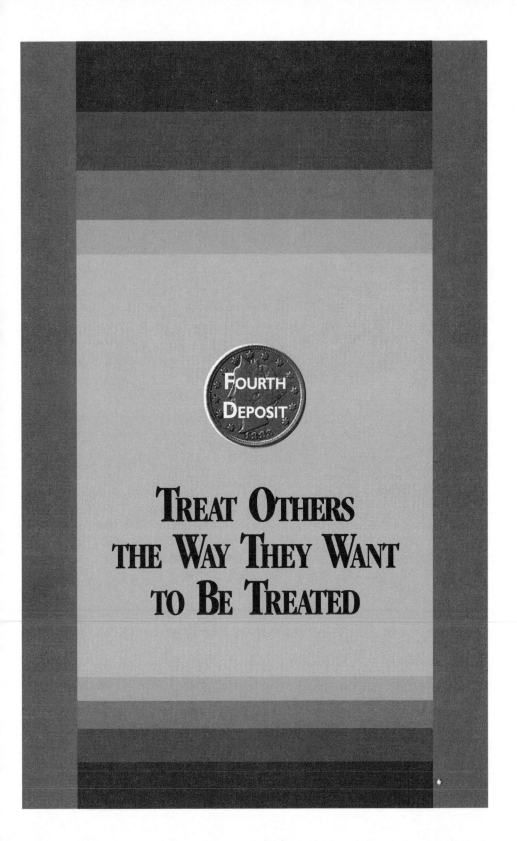

FOURTH DEPOSIT:
TREAT OTHERS THE WAY
THEY WANT TO BE TREATED

You can always spot a well-informed man — his views are the same as yours.

ILKA CHASE

A CHIP OFF THE OLD BLOCK

eople handle crisis differently. People handle life differently. While my belief is that each individual is created with a uniqueness that sets him apart from all others, people have tendencies that can group them together regarding their style of behavior and communication. The more we know about ourselves and others, the better we are able to handle a crisis. The better we are able to handle life.

In August 1993 my family and I set out for a three-week adventure in Europe. My parents, in-laws, husband, two sons, and I took a ferry and train from Copenhagen, Denmark, to Essen, Germany. The train arrived twenty-five minutes late. We had planned to rent vans to get to our prepaid rooms in an expensive hotel in the next town. The van rental company was closed; so was the American Consulate. There we stood at the train station, eight stranded people with sixteen pieces of luggage, in a part of Germany where nobody spoke English.

I find it interesting to look back at how we each handled the crisis. Our common goal was to arrive, safely and within a reasonable time, at our hotel. I stood in the train station office trying to explain our plight to uncomprehending officials and demanding that someone contact the van rental store. My mother and my father-in-law assured me that everything would work out just fine. My husband and his mother concerned themselves with details. The boys were hungry — they just wanted something to eat, and fast. My father laughed and talked about what a great memory this would make.

It was a classic learning experience. I learned that it doesn't do much good to make demands in a country where you don't even speak the language. My children learned that hunger pains eventually go away. My husband and mother-in-law learned much about the area through studying maps, and eventually they came up with the solution. My mother and father-in-law were right — everything did work out (after a $200 taxi ride). My father was right, too: this day, September 13, 1993, made quite a memory for us all.

As a family we knew and understood one another well, so we were able to communicate effectively and accomplish our collective mission. Not all people thrown together in a crisis are so fortunate.

Through understanding, we have an opportunity to adapt to others and thus increase the effectiveness of communication. Understanding people helps us make the fourth deposit in the Four Deposits For Balance: Treat others the way they want to be treated.

●●●●●●●●●●●●●●●

A BRIEF HISTORY OF BEHAVIORAL STYLES

For centuries, hoping to learn how to reduce conflict and increase effective communication, philosophers and scientists have sought the keys to human behavior. As early as 444 BC, Empedocles theorized that everything was made up of four elements: earth, air, fire, and water. A half century later, Hippocrates held that climate and terrain affected behavior; he also identified four temperaments and associated them with four bodily fluids or "humors." Galen (AD 130–200) thought that these four bodily fluids had a definite effect on behavior. Twentieth-century scientists, such as Germany's C. G. Jung, identified four personality types based on their ways of thinking, feeling, sensation, and intuition.

Harvard graduate William Moulton Marston (1893–1947) made a major contribution to understanding behavioral style: he was the principal developer of the DISC language. In *The Emotions of Normal People* (1928), he classified people by their dominance, inducement, submissiveness, and compliance. Walter Clark, in the 1950s, was the first person to develop an instrument based on Marston's theory. Over the last forty-seven years, many other scientists have perfected this instrument and continued the research. The terms in common use now for these four behavior types are Dominant, Influential, Steady, and Compliant.

A Fast Trip
Around the Block

Have you ever been told you're a "chip off the old block"? Well, in a way, each of us is a chip off the old block — the block of human behavior.

Think of all human behavior types as being represented by a block:

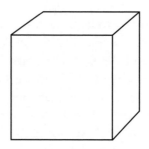

Let's divide this block in half from top to bottom:

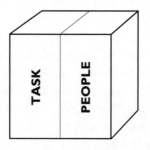

Now let's say arbitrarily that persons on the left side of the block are very task oriented. Their function in life is to accomplish objectives, and their main purpose in communicating is to get the job done. Task-oriented people are not people haters; they get along just fine as long as people

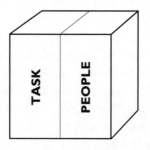 TASK   PEOPLE

TREAT OTHERS THE WAY THEY WANT

are getting the job done. Otherwise, task-oriented people have no use for them.

Persons on the right side of the block are people oriented. Their goal in life is to establish relationships. They use communication as a tool to accomplish this. They can be very sociable, but they get the job done as long as people are around them to help. After all, what's the use of a task if not to build rapport with people?

Well, so far, which side of the block are you on? Are you more task oriented or people oriented? Most people have some characteristics of both parts. If this is a hard decision for you, you may have approximately equal amounts of both sides in you.

Let's cut the block another way — from left to right:

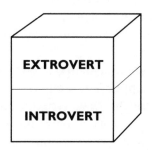

This time we'll specify that people in the top half are extroverts. Extroverts like to be in the limelight, the center of attention. If you don't give them attention, they find ways to get it. Extroverts are the people who speak up readily in group meetings. They like to take charge and lead, and they crave all the fanfare that comes with leadership.

People in the lower half of the block are introverts. Introverts prefer a support role rather than a leading role. You won't find them in the spotlight if they have anything to say about it. Quiet and reserved, they prefer to work behind the scenes. Are you an extrovert or an introvert? If you're like most, you tend one way or the other but have some characteristics of both types.

Now let's take a look with the block cut both ways:

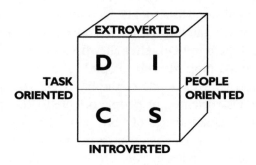

The upper left quadrant represents the task-oriented extrovert; upper right, the people-oriented extrovert; lower right, the people-oriented introvert; lower left, the task-oriented introvert.

Notice that we've assigned a letter to each quadrant: clockwise from upper left, they are D, I, S, and C. This is the framework for the DISC system of behavioral classification, which we'll explain below. But for convenience in our discussion, we'll make a couple of other changes. First we will give each of the quadrants a different color, like this:

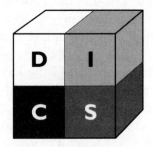

Then, for reasons you'll understand later, we'll disassemble the block and rearrange the four quadrants side by side in a single row, like this:

DISCovering Behavioral and Communication Styles

Let's take a closer look at the quadrants in our personality block. What do the letters D, I, S, and C stand for?

W hat's in a Personality?

D	I	S	C
Dominant	Influential	Steady	Compliant
Driving	Impulsive	Stable	Conscientious
Daring	Introducer	Shy	Cautious
Doer	Impetuous	Security	Competent
Dynamic	Interested	Supportive	Careful
Dramatic	Illogical	Spectator	Calculating
Demanding	Interesting	Sweet	Critical Thinker
Dogmatic	Inconsistent	Submissive	Consistent
Dictator	Inspirational	Succor	Correct
Defiant	Impressionable	Sentimental	Conformist
Direct	Important	Status Quo	Control

In the following chapters we will discuss these behaviors in detail. Basically, however, this list indicates that a person who is, say, demanding, defiant, direct, and dogmatic is most likely to be a Dominant personality; another way of saying this is that he has a "High D" personality. Someone who is usually sweet, sentimental, supportive, and shy would probably be considered a "High S" person.

Most people, however, have some characteristics of each component — personality traits that they display or hide, depending on the circumstances. Most of us have strong traits in at least two of the quadrants. My personality is fairly high in the Dominant and Influential components, low in the Steady, and middle-of-the-road in Compliant.

If I take a knife and, measuring from the bottom of each quadrant, make a cut that represents how much of each quadrant is represented in my personality, the result looks like this:

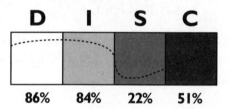

And here's what my chip looks like by itself:

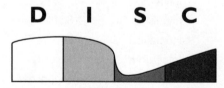

Every individual in the world has a unique chip — a personality that is not exactly like that of any other person on earth. What does your chip look like? The next four chapters will help you answer this question in terms of behavior and communication style. This insight will help you learn how to communicate effectively with other personality types.

●●●●●●●●●●●●●●●

WHAT'S NOT IN YOUR CHIP

It's important to understand that the DISC model does *not* account for all the factors that go into and shape an individual's personality — in particular:

- intelligence,
- moral values,
- education,
- experience, and
- age.

Two individuals with similar behavioral profiles can easily end up pursuing very different goals and living radically different lives because of differences in intelligence, moral values, education, experience, and age. Adolf Hitler and Martin Luther King Jr. had arguably similar behavior profiles — dominating, daring, direct, influential, impressionable — but vast differences in experiences and moral values sent them down totally different tracks.

Some behavior researchers have chosen to include intelligence as a behavior trait. This is almost certainly false; certain personality types are more driven to learn, others have a greater need to obtain information, but native intelligence is not the driving factor in these tendencies. It does, however, increase the likelihood of success in our endeavors. Similarly, our experience, education, and age continually modify our behavior and influence the results of our actions. For example, as we mature we generally become calmer. For some personality types, this is beneficial; for others, it may be detrimental.

As we study and discuss the different personalities and behavior styles in the next four chapters, remember the following facts about the DISC model we are using:

- The DISC model does not measure or represent a person's intelligence.

- The DISC model does not measure or represent a person's experience.

- The DISC model does not measure or represent a person's moral values.

- The DISC model does not measure or represent an individual's education.

Having sufficiently covered these exceptions, let's take a close and detailed look at each of the four basic personality types.

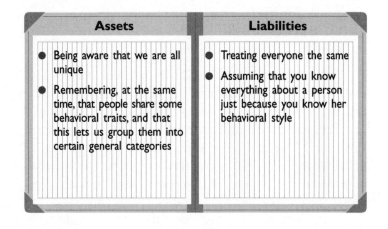

Assets	Liabilities
• Being aware that we are all unique • Remembering, at the same time, that people share some behavioral traits, and that this lets us group them into certain general categories	• Treating everyone the same • Assuming that you know everything about a person just because you know her behavioral style

You can only see others as clearly as you see yourself.

STEPHEN C. PAUL

It's better to be a lion for a day
than a sheep all your life.

SISTER ELIZABETH KENNY

20

THE DOMINANT
PERSONALITY

The fourth deposit in the Four Deposits for Balance is this: Treat others the way they want to be treated. It's pretty important to remember this principle when you're dealing with the kind of person we discuss in this chapter: the Dominant type. If you don't, he'll probably have you for lunch.

A few years ago I was vice president of an association of business owners whose board meetings often lasted longer than necessary. Knowing my inclination to keep meetings on task, the board president — a High D type — asked me to help keep board members on track. I pursued my assignment with relish. During one board meeting, the discussion on a certain subject had gone on far too long. Paying no heed to the fact that it was the president herself who was dominating the discussion, I pointed out how much time we had spent on the issue and how little remained in the meeting. I suggested that we move on. The president looked directly at me and said, "Perhaps you'd like to be president, Beverly, and come sit in this chair." Meeting her gaze with my own, I assured her that was not my desire.

High D's are driven, direct, and controlling. They recognize one another easily and quickly become locked in competition. Keeping this competition under control usually requires a formal pecking order — president, vice president, and so forth — to set boundaries on the degree of conflict that will be tolerated.

TRAITS OF A HIGH D

High D's are decisive. They have no difficulty arriving at a decision or opinion. This can be both a strength and a liability. Their ability in a crisis to make a quick decision, even a bad one, is a great advantage in this fast-paced world. The liability is that a High D may make the decision before she gets all the information, and so is more likely to make mistakes. Errors don't set High D's back, however; their motto is "Win some, lose some." They simply drive on to the next task and the next decision. Their ability to reverse course quickly and move on often leaves confusion in their wake.

High D's are egotistical, and although ego is popularly considered a negative trait, there's nothing wrong about feeling good about yourself. Their competence and self-confidence is a strength; only when it's proclaimed to others does it become a negative.

High D's like to take risks. They're not afraid to bet the family farm: "Nothing ventured, nothing gained." Their experience and intelligence largely determine how successful the risk taking will be.

High D's are impatient. Initially we read this as a negative trait, because they can be quite demanding — they want everything done yesterday. But it is this very impatience that drives them to accomplish so much. Without the urgency of the High D's, we might still be riding around in buggies.

High D's are competitive. They like to win. They enjoy a fair fight. People who participate in competitive sports either have this High D trait or quickly develop it.

High D's are task oriented. They keep their focus on the job at hand and pay little attention to people around them unless they get in the way. This sometimes gives the false impression that they dislike people.

High D's are confrontational. If they have a problem with you, you'll soon know it; they don't hesitate or wait for the ideal moment to tell you what you did wrong. This intimidating, confrontational style often makes other behavior types pale at their approach. The confrontation may be emotionally charged or not. When the High D becomes angry, he'll forget his anger once he's had his say. A High D doesn't hold a grudge; he's gotten over yesterday's confrontation and thinks you have, too.

STRENGTHS OF THE HIGH D

High D's are fast organizers. If you need something done quickly, give it to your highest D. She will not only meet deadlines, she'll meet them with an organized plan. Getting the task done and getting it done on deadline is the focus of the High D. Granted, anyone who gets in her way may end up sitting on the sidelines licking his wounds.

High D's are time efficient. This is one of the reasons they can accomplish so much. In a meeting, D's don't get distracted; in fact, they can seem quite blunt in staying focused on the agenda.

High D's achieve deadlines. If a High D tells you she'll have it to you by Monday morning, you can sleep Sunday night knowing that you'll have it the next day. In a work setting, the D may replace slow people, causing bafflement and injured feelings. They mean nothing personal by this; it's just a matter of getting the job done.

High D's like to improve things. Even if everything is going well, they think it could be even better. Others may perceive them as restless; they see themselves as progressive and forward looking.

My older sister is a High D. As a teenager, she didn't have many outlets for her drive, so she took out her need to control on our shared bedroom. It was not uncommon for her to rearrange the furniture weekly. I couldn't get up in the middle of the night without bumping into something. Now, every time I visit her home in Ohio, the rooms are different. I don't mean she's changed the color scheme or the wallpaper, I mean the rooms are different — what was the office is now the playroom. In fact, she changes the functions of the rooms so often that my parents and I refer to the rooms by location, such as the "front right room."

High D's are results oriented. Managers in authority know they can rely on High D's to get things done quickly.

Therefore, at least on paper, High D's accomplish a great deal.

High D's are responsible. They readily acknowledge mistakes and immediately set out to correct them. If a subordinate commits an error, the High D will take the blame with his superior and deal with the subordinate later.

High D's overcome obstacles. When they encounter one, they go over, under, around, or straight through it — or you, if you're in the way. The song that goes, "Ain't no mountain high enough . . ." could have been written by a High D. Some become so focused on finding a way past an obstacle that, even as they succeed, they let other aspects of their lives get out of control.

MAJOR WEAKNESSES
OF THE HIGH D

High D's lack people skills. They will use fear, if necessary, to get you to focus on the task. They want the job done, and if they have to hurt your feelings to get it done, so be it. Nothing personal, of course, but after all, "nice guys finish last." However, with demand for people-oriented managers rising in the U.S., many High D's are learning to control their tempers and treat their people more courteously.

> The major weakness of High D's is their lack of people skills.

High D's are in a hurry. They sometimes move so quickly that they don't get all the information they need before acting. Because they don't mind making mistakes, High D's are often heedless of their effects on others. Many find their ability to "turn on a dime" unsettling.

NEEDS OF THE HIGH D

High D's seek challenges. If no problems or opportunities present themselves, a High D will often create one. This doesn't mean sabotage; it means the High D may take a risk in hopes of either a big gain or an opportunity to fix something.

High D's need variety. They don't do well in an environment where everything stays the same; they feel compelled to shake up the operation and watch where everything settles — to put their mark on it.

I have a client whose wife's family owned a beautiful antebellum mansion in a southern town. The house was inherited by the owner's oldest son, who happened to be a High D. Although he valued his mother's tradition, he quite simply didn't like where the house was. He paid a small fortune to have it moved to another location and restored to its former glory. High D's just can't leave things alone, even if the thing is the address of a home.

High D's crave power. They need to be in a position of authority. Give D's power and watch them soar.

O ne client of mine, a High D, was an inside consultant — a position that, although prestigious, gave him no authority in the company. He could make recommendations, but no one had to listen to him or do what he said. Nevertheless, he kept the company in constant turmoil with his impatience and his tendency toward confrontation. Eventually he got a chance to become a plant manager. Although this was a lateral transfer away from headquarters, I realized that it would be an opportunity for him to shine. Soon my other clients in this company began telling me how well this man was adjusting and communicating. I smiled. The High D had finally landed a position of power, even if in a small kingdom. The division president reportedly said to this High D, "I've finally found something you can do."

High D's need independence. They do not work well for a manager who is constantly looking over their shoulder. It's best to give them the bottom line, then step back and allow them to accomplish it their way. This need for independence is one reason so many High D's become entrepreneurs.

GOAL OF THE HIGH D

The goal of the High D is quite simple: to control. He wants to control the situation, the finances, the outcome, and you. Others look at him and think of him as a control freak; the High D sees himself as simply one who is willing to step up to the plate.

EMOTIONS OF THE HIGH D

For task-oriented communicators, High D's can be quite emotional — and the emotion you see is only the tip of the iceberg. Hidden beneath the surface is a much larger and more complex set of feelings. If you see anger, you can be fairly sure that beneath his anger the High D is hiding the pain of a past injury — for instance, being passed over for a promotion that he thought he deserved. His ego and self-esteem are damaged. Underlying the pain is fear; if he didn't get the promotion, maybe he's going nowhere in this corporation. Or worse: "Will I continue to have a job with this company?"

Eventually the High D will need to forgive himself and others for all real or imagined injuries. Only then will he experience the characteristic High D sense of well-being, which is the largest hidden part of the iceberg.

How to Lead the High D

It's not easy to get a High D to follow your lead; it's a real challenge, because he wants to be the leader. It's important to define the rules and clearly explain to him the results you expect. You'll also need to provide assignments that are challenging and intriguing. Establish a plan of advancement and career movement so the High D can see where he's going; otherwise you may lose a valuable employee. You'll also need to provide the High D with some specific training, including, but certainly not limited to, listening, understanding teamwork, group dynamics, people skills, and communication. With these tools the High D can achieve great success.

> Allow the High D to fail. Even if he's having trouble, don't take him off the job.

Allow the High D to fail. This is important. Falling short of accomplishing the task is very humbling for the High D; it may even break him. Therefore, even if he's having trouble, don't take him off the job. Get him back on his horse, and hold him accountable by keeping him on the job until he succeeds. This will help him develop his skill at overcoming obstacles. Don't chastise him, because there's nothing you can say to him that he hasn't already told himself. If you handle him right, both you and the High D will profit from the experience. He will gain a better understanding of his own faults and limitations, and he'll learn to appreciate the value of working with others to accomplish the end result. You will have helped him become a valuable leader.

TREAT OTHERS THE WAY THEY WANT

HOW THE HIGH D WANTS TO BE TREATED

Give the bottom line. Do it as quickly as possible to keep the High D's attention. Don't try her patience by dwelling on minute details; they're not important to her, and she won't listen.

Look for a win-win outcome. Although a High D enjoys a challenging problem or task, she does not like to be personally challenged. When confronting or negotiating with a High D, remember to let her win some of the arguments. This will help you in the long run, because you'll probably have to interact with her later. At the same time, remember this: hold your ground. If your drive or dominance is not as strong as hers, you'll quickly find yourself on the losing end.

Start the conversation with business. Don't bother with small talk about hobbies, the weather, her family; the High D prefers to focus on the task and get it done. If it makes you more comfortable to be sociable, at least keep it short. If you ask how she is and she says, "Fine," leave it at that. She does not wish to establish a friendship; she wishes to get the work done.

Ask "what" questions. These will gain you more information from the High D than a yes/no question, but her answers won't be as long or laborious as for a "how" question, and she doesn't really want to waste time giving you all the details anyway. She may also regard the "why" question as a challenge to her authority or ability.

Give information, not opinion. She won't attack if you give her information she didn't have. Of course, if she asks for your opinion, by all means give it. But if you volunteer an opinion, she may well counter with her own, and suddenly you're wasting time arguing. If an opinion is necessary, don't be afraid to take a stand; still, show that your opinion is based on information: "According to the data we collected last quarter, it seems obvious to me that . . ."

Don't be intimidated; maintain your dominance. Don't try to become more dominant than you normally are, just hold steady on course. Sit up straight, look her in the eye, answer her questions. When you maintain your dominance, you'll find that the High D tiger does not attack as readily.

I n a meeting I had with a president of a large service organization, I soon saw that he was a High D. With me he was quite cordial and obviously a very intelligent man — a High D under control. Then we went into his management team meeting. Suddenly this controlled High D came unglued. I noticed that one of his managers sat with his head down, trying to avoid his glare. It didn't work. This president chewed him up and spit him out.

Be prepared and organized when interacting with the High D. Don't be spontaneous or off the cuff. High D's are task-oriented communicators; they like to take action based on facts, not feelings.

Be decisive; don't sit on the fence. A High D would rather you be wrong than gutless. When she asks for your opinion, have one to give.

Keep your voice down. Don't catch the High D's anger; she can easily increase her volume and pitch, which can lead to a shouting match. Purposely lower the pitch and volume of your voice to keep things calm. You'll function better that way.

Be logical rather than emotional with a High D. Getting all choked up or tearful is not effective. Postpone communication until you can keep your emotions in check.

Expect direct rejection from a High D. She will quickly tell you no without explanation. Whatever you do, don't get defensive. She's not rejecting you; your idea simply doesn't fit her plan for the task. Don't cave in, though. Control the discussion systematically: accept the rejection unemotionally, use a StartProbe to get an explanation, interject neutral comments, listen carefully, and bring the discussion to a controlled stop. (This is a good time to review chapter 18.)

Be clear and explicit in your meaning. Don't imply or hint at anything; the High D may well miss it. Don't tell her something is okay while your body and voice are signaling that it's anything but okay. The High D will hear the words, and the underlying message that you're not in full agreement will be lost.

Don't interrupt her. She will take this as a challenge to her authority or knowledge. Instead, when she says something you disagree with, pause, and perhaps make a slow body movement to release some of your tension, but allow her to continue. There will be a time for you to give your information, but for now it's important to the High D's ego that you pay attention while she's speaking.

SELLING A SERVICE, IDEA, OR PRODUCT TO THE HIGH D

Get right down to business. Refrain from talking about anything off task. Begin by asking questions, especially "what" questions, to determine what need the High D has for your service, idea, or product. Then give him only the required information.

Honor his time. Hit the high points and get to the bottom line. If you have five selling points, give your strongest points up front. The High D is a quick decision maker; he may decide before you get to point five.

Avoid using research data and testimonials. This is a lot of information and detail that, quite simply, does not interest the D. You can easily lose a sale by overselling your service, idea, or product to the High D.

Show this individual new products, new services, and new ideas. Remember that the High D likes risk and change. To be the first company to use your product, idea, or service can be very appealing to the High D.

Appear credible and organized. Demonstrate to the High D that you manage your time well and that you're prepared. Don't fumble around looking for some bit of information that doesn't interest the High D in the first place.

Give direct answers. If you don't know the answer, tell him that you don't know and that you'll find out and get the information to him. Give him a specific time: "I don't have the information to answer that question adequately. I'll get back to you by four o'clock this afternoon."

Ask for the High D's opinion. He'll probably give it to you anyway. By asking for it, you retain some control of the conversation. Handle any rejection calmly and systematically, using StartProbes to gain information. Listen carefully.

In a selling situation, statements like the following might motivate this dominant, direct, daring, High D person to buy from you:

"You're the type of person who can be successful with this."

"This puts you on the cutting edge of your industry."

"This is totally new."

"This will increase your efficiency by ___ percent."

THE BOTTOM LINE

Approximately 18 percent of the population in the United States has D as the dominant behavior trait. Remember, they're looking for results; anything you can do to help them achieve their results quickly and efficiently will be welcomed.

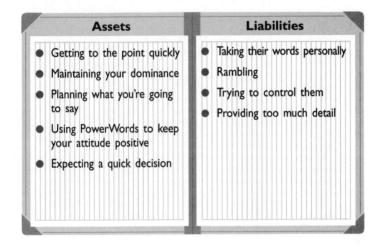

Assets	Liabilities
● Getting to the point quickly	● Taking their words personally
● Maintaining your dominance	● Rambling
● Planning what you're going to say	● Trying to control them
● Using PowerWords to keep your attitude positive	● Providing too much detail
● Expecting a quick decision	

Progress always involves risk. You can't steal second base and keep your foot on first.

FREDERICK B. WILCOX

A wise man knows everything;
a shrewd one knows everybody.

ANONYMOUS

THE INFLUENTIAL
PERSONALITY

eople with a high In-
fluential personality
component are per-
sonable extroverts, in
their element handling people and running the show.
They may make you dizzy with their whirlwind activities.
To have balance in your people account with the High I,
you need to understand her spontaneity, her ability to make
quick decisions, and her zest for life.

In October 1996, my longtime companion and best friend died. His name was Hershey. He was a chocolate standard poodle. I grieved for weeks. Finally, one day I told Ken, my husband, that I felt ready to get another dog. He agreed and suggested I begin looking for one.

Ken left town the next day on business. I called the breeder in New York who had sold me Hershey. I was delighted to hear that she had apricots and silvers. They were too young to ship, but I could certainly come and get one. I checked the calendar. The upcoming weekend was a brief window of opportunity in my busy schedule. I called my travel agent and picked up the airline tickets.

That evening on the phone I told Ken that I was leaving Saturday morning to get the dog. He was astounded: wasn't I moving just a little too fast on this? Perhaps he's right, I thought. I called the travel agent and canceled my tickets.

The next morning, Ken called to check on my travel plans. I told him I had canceled. Again he was amazed: hadn't I changed my mind rather quickly? I should just do what I wanted, he said. Again I called the travel agent (High I's are a travel agent's nightmare) and rebooked the flight. Within three days I was holding an adorable, fluffy, apricot standard poodle in my arms.

People with High I behavioral style are impulsive, excitable, influential and easily influenced, and they have a lot of fun with life because of their optimism. Let's take a closer look at their specific behavior traits.

TRAITS OF THE HIGH I

High I's are excitable. Not just things that excite you and me — everything is exciting for an I. Sometimes the excitement of a High I is very catching; no one else can motivate you quite this way. Unfortunately, when the High I is in a downswing mood, it's evident to everyone around them that something is wrong.

High I's are influential. They can convince you that your brown walls are green or that you absolutely have a distinct need for a particular service, idea, or product. Some of the things they talk you into are very beneficial for you. Other times they will persuade you to do something that is not in your best interest.

High I's are well liked. They know a lot of people. When they throw a party, they can easily invite over a hundred people. They are friendly and outgoing, and because they seek name recognition, a lot of people know who they are.

High I's are promoters. They are good at promoting ideas, products, and services — not only their own, but yours as well. This is a wonderful trait, except when they promote something that they know little about; then they can come across as shallow.

High I's are people oriented. They can find something to like about everyone they meet, and no one is a stranger. If you need to find a qualified person for your project, talk with a High I; he will probably know just the right person, or at least someone who can find her for you.

High I's are trusting. They expect people to be above board, honest, and true. You have their trust until you abuse it, and even when someone goes astray, the High I's first impulse is to look for an explanation and give her a second and third chance. As a manager of people, it is hard for the High I to admit when it's finally time to cut the losses. The High I always believes the pot of gold is just over the next hill.

High I's are fast problem solvers. Like High D's, they can change their minds quickly when they get new information or opinions from someone they like. Spontaneous and impulsive, they reverse course readily — a trait that can be quite disruptive to other behavioral styles.

STRENGTHS OF THE HIGH I

High I's are creative. They stretch the envelope. They are free thinkers; coloring outside the lines is their specialty. Confronted with problems, they can come up with solutions no one has ever thought of before. Although these solutions might seem a bit strange, don't discount them until they've been tried.

High I's have a sense of humor. They like to get laughs and are often skilled at reducing tension with well-timed quips. This can indeed be a strength, unless the High I uses humor as a mask. Whenever I counsel High I's who overuse humor, I caution them that although humor may have served them well initially, they need to move beyond that tendency.

In a seminar I was conducting, one person kept us all in stitches. Everything he said was funny. I quickly realized he was using humor as a shield, even in serious situations. Alone with him later, I asked him if he had a problem with people not taking him seriously. He admitted that he did but that he'd been cracking jokes so long he didn't know how to stop. I asked him to share this need with other members of the group; later he did so. He learned that it's okay to be humorous — just not all the time.

High I's are good speakers. They have the gift of gab. These are people who can get up in front of customers and put on an impressive performance. Their excellent speaking skills are one reason they can be so persuasive. However, they are usually not the best listeners; they'd rather talk.

High I's are negotiators. Because they can read and understand people so well, they are excellent at negotiating win-win solutions to conflicts. They can be smooth talkers, and yet they can do this with great sincerity. Most people are like putty in their hands.

High I's are motivators. Most of the world's great leaders have had excellent motivational skills. Recently our entire training staff attended a one-day motivational seminar in Knoxville, Tennessee, to hear Zig Ziglar, Robert Schuller, and other inspirational speakers. As I sat there listening, I realized they were indeed High I's. Did they motivate us? Did they make us want to be the very best we could be? Of course they did, in true High I fashion.

High I's are team leaders. They know how to motivate, to control talkative team members, and to draw out the quiet ones; they know when silence means disapproval. They can be good leaders because they understand people — and teams are, after all, made up of people.

High I's handle change well. They don't match High D's as agents of change, but they're probably the most flexible people walking the earth. One corporation where I have many clients recently underwent a change in management. Of the twenty or so individuals I was working with, only the High I's adjusted without apparent stress. They would say, "Oh, it's all going to work out," or "They just have a different way of doing things." High D's make change; High I's handle change.

Major Weaknesses of the High I

High I's lack follow-through. They have excellent intentions, and they say yes to many people. Unfortunately, perhaps because they have so many irons in the fire and because their focus is on people rather than tasks, they tend to leave things undone. Most High I's need to be trained in planning, managing time, and accomplishing goals, or they should be teamed with people with good organizational skills. Tools such as electronic organizers and daily planners are helpful to the High I only if she learns to use them regularly.

High I's are impulsive. Although this makes their life exciting, it can also land them in the poorhouse.

A relative of mine, who is a very High I, didn't buy one boat, he bought two. (Actually, he didn't buy either boat; he negotiated for them.) He also bought a riding lawnmower. Unfortunately, his yard was so small and steep he could never use it. Impulsive buying and instant gratification are trademarks of a High I.

●●●●●●●●●●●●●●●

NEEDS OF THE HIGH I

High I's need recognition. They crave attention; they like to see their names in print. If they've done something out of the ordinary, they like the boss to point them out in front of all of their co-workers and to have them stand up and be applauded. Other behavior types consider this need somewhat infantile; for the High I, it fulfills a need. A High I's motto might be "It doesn't matter what they say about you, just so they spell your name right."

Because of this need for recognition, High I's use the pronoun "I" more often than "we." They don't do this to take credit for the work of others, but because they believe that without their ideas and influence it would not have been done. They may well be correct.

High I's need a friendly environment. They do not thrive where everything is all work and no play. They prefer to spice things up with celebrations — birthdays, holidays, or anything else that comes to mind. Make sure the workplace is a fun place; otherwise, you'll often find the High I off task, talking to people and generally making his own fun.

If you need to plan a company picnic or Christmas party, call in the High I; he'll love the assignment. Just make sure you put a task-oriented communicator with him to follow though on the details.

Finally, I's need freedom. They don't do well when tied down by seemingly unnecessary rules and regulations. Tell them the goal and give them the freedom to reach it in their own way. As long as they're allowed to tap into their creativity, they can be exceptional workers.

THE GOAL OF THE HIGH I

The goal of the High I is simple: it is to influence. He wants you to agree with him, to admire his ideas and accomplishments, to do what he suggests, to like what he likes and dislike what he dislikes. It's fascinating to watch a High I in upper management bring others over to his way of thinking. However, a High I can be too influential; those being persuaded may get so caught up in the High I's enthusiasm that they fail to question the wisdom of his ideas.

EMOTIONS OF A HIGH I

The greatest of the High I's many powerful emotions is optimism. She feels that everything will work out, even when the situation looks bleak: "Every cloud has a silver lining." Such optimism is catching; it can be very effective when a team is struggling with motivation. Sometimes, however, the High I's optimism is unrealistic and can leave her and others unprepared to face reality.

How to Lead the High I

A High I will work well for a leader who recognizes and is comfortable with her creativity, who can be flexible in working with her, and who gives her goals that take advantage of her person-to-person and speaking skills. Don't lock her away in a room with a machine; give her information, put her among people, and let her be an influencer. Encourage her to be the best she can be.

At the same time, a High I needs a leader who can anchor her, like a string does a kite, without bringing her crashing to the ground; who helps her set realistic goals; and who, while remaining flexible, provides deadlines for her to meet. A High I will work best for a leader who is friendly, who interacts with her every day, and who keeps the door open so she can discuss items important to her at any time.

How an I Wants to Be Treated

First, listen. The High I likes to talk; you'll get along with him best if you let him. Instead of interrupting, jot down notes on points to cover when your turn to talk finally comes around. You can then control the conversation by asking him questions that lead him to talk about things you want to discuss.

Don't change topics abruptly; instead, use a bridging remark to get him back to business. For instance, if he's rambling on and on about golf, say, "Speaking of hitting the mark, how close are we to the goal of obtaining four new clients this month?" The High I will usually take your lead and change the topic to the work subject. An abrupt change of topic would alarm him; his first thought would be that

TREAT OTHERS THE WAY THEY WANT

you need to lighten up. Until you can demonstrate that you're a sociable creature, he will strive to turn you into one.

Provide a friendly environment. Don't be all business. Start the conversation with social talk. Ask him about his family and his roles outside of work. This will endear you to him, and because he's people oriented, he'll do more to please you.

Hit the high points; don't get bogged down in details with the High I. Remember, he's a bottom-line person and likes to take a broad view of things.

Expect a quick decision from the High I, and be prepared to firm it up immediately. You may think you have him saying yes, but unless you affirm the decision, it may not turn into a reality. Use a closed question, such as a ParaProbe, at the end of a conversation: "So you're going to call Mr. Brown by this afternoon, right?"

Get him involved emotionally. Bring your personality to the conversation. A little charm on your part will go a long way toward getting the High I to agree with you. High I's are influential, but they can also be influenced.

Give the High I stories and names, not just cold facts. When trying to get him to see your side of it, illustrate it with a real or hypothetical example. This reaches his personal side and gets him emotionally involved.

Recognize his accomplishments. Whatever you do, never belittle a High I, especially in front of others. It's best not to belittle anyone, of course, but doing so can severely damage the ego of the High I. He may never recover from it and may avoid you thereafter.

Sell your idea, product, or service to the High I, don't just recite facts to him. You'll get a lot further if you try to engage his emotions in the deal.

Ask for input. Gather ideas from the High I rather than presenting a finished proposal. If you have his buy-in, he's more likely to do what you want him to.

Promote action from the High I. He can be a terrific dreamer and thinker, but it's important for him to take those dreams and thoughts and turn them into action. Listen to his dreams, then ask him how he plans to accomplish them. Be ready with a note pad; jot down his plan and present it to him in writing afterwards. This will help ensure that his dreams become reality.

Recognize his persuasive power. Never underestimate the ability of the High I to persuade you to do something you may not need or want to do. Remember, a High I can sell snow to an Eskimo. One way to hold that persuasive power in check is to ask for information or verification. This requires him to be slightly more task oriented.

SELLING TO THE HIGH I

Selling to a High I can be a lot of fun, as long as you remember the following points.

Be personable. Don't be all business. The High I likes dealing with people, not just facts or issues. Get her involved emotionally. Tell her stories.

Spare excessive detail. Hit the high points. Get to the bottom line quickly. Remember, she's a quick decision maker.

Listen to her. Don't do all the talking. When you need to concentrate on a particular subject, don't be too abrupt — use a bridge to get back on topic.

Support her dreams. If you're a task-oriented communicator or an organized person, take her dreams and turn them into a plan for success.

Use testimonials. She loves the personal involvement and the human interaction of hearing how other people accomplish success.

Follow up on any item discussed. After the meeting, send her a brief memo outlining your agreement.

The High I is easily motivated. Statements like these might help you sell to this creative and influential person:

"I'd like to showcase your business with this product or service."

"Many people are attracted to this but most settle for less."

"You'd be one of the first!"

FRIENDLY PERSUASION

High I's constitute approximately 28 percent of the population in the United States. They like to buy showy or new products. They're looking for the experience of buying from you; if they enjoy it, they'll do it again.

Talk is certainly not cheap with High I's. If you let them, they'll talk too much and cost you time. If you forget to show them warmth, it may cost you the relationship. If they don't follow through, it can cost you money.

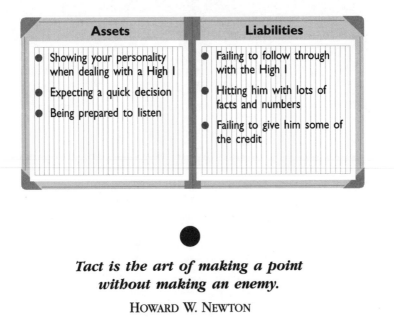

Assets	Liabilities
• Showing your personality when dealing with a High I	• Failing to follow through with the High I
• Expecting a quick decision	• Hitting him with lots of facts and numbers
• Being prepared to listen	• Failing to give him some of the credit

Tact is the art of making a point without making an enemy.

HOWARD W. NEWTON

*To be humble to superiors is a duty, to equals
courtesy, to inferiors nobleness.*

BENJAMIN FRANKLIN

THE STEADY
PERSONALITY

I t can be very impor-
tant to have balance
in your people ac-
count with the High S
because these people do not like to change, and that can
include changing the way they think about you. These
warm introverts remain "steady as she goes," even in some
quite exciting situations.

I have a dear friend who helped me raise my children. For ten and a half years she was their nanny. She provided a loving environment for the boys, both in our home and at the office.

Besides the children, Nanny and I have something else in common: our love of Southeastern Conference Football. Her team of choice is the Alabama Crimson Tide, mine the Tennessee Volunteers. One year, when Alabama played Tennessee in Knoxville, I got tickets on the forty-yard line in the alumni section. I was excited, eager for revenge. Although her team had beaten mine in each of the last seven years, I just knew that this day would be the day we turned the Tide.

It was a well-fought game, and the score stayed close. But in the last quarter, with only minutes to go, Alabama sneaked ahead with a touchdown pass. I was devastated. Out of the corner of my eye I caught Nanny on her feet — but in a strange posture. She looked as though she had been caught between two elevator doors. I realized that she was quietly, very quietly, celebrating her victory.

On the way home, she spoke not one word about how her team had beaten my team yet again. I knew she was being kind and considerate — in typical S fashion.

●●●●●●●●●●●●●●●●

TRAITS OF THE HIGH S

High S's are stable. This makes them good listeners who let the other person talk while they provide a safe environ-

ment for communication. Sometimes, however, people will take advantage of their willingness to listen. When I go out to dinner with a certain friend of mine who has High S traits, it's as though she has "listener" stamped in bold letters on her forehead. Odds are we'll end up with a waitress telling my friend her life story. Because they are so willing to listen, S's often internalize whatever they hear. They seem unable to shrug it off. Spending a lot of time listening, especially on topics not related to work, can also decrease their productivity.

High S's are cooperative. They like agreement and harmony. If they can, they'll go along with you. This makes them nice people. It also means that sometimes they don't share their ideas, which hurts not only them but the whole family or work team. They need to be encouraged to speak up.

High S's are patient. They're not pushy or demanding. They'll wait patiently for you to come to a decision. This sounds like a wonderful trait, but sometimes the S may be too patient. For instance, the High S supervisor may ask one of his employees for a report. When it doesn't come, the supervisor goes to check on it. The employee needs more time. The supervisor waits patiently; he may be fuming inside, but outwardly he's the picture of patience. The result? Productivity declines and frustration rises.

High S's are loyal. Their loyalty is not just for family and close friends, it extends to their work team, their company, even their retailers.

I n our neighborhood there's a drug store that has been around as long as I can remember. It's not the largest or the most modern, but a friend of mine continues to frequent this drug store. Even when a new drug store with more space, better selection, and lower prices opened across the street, my friend stayed with the old. Was it because she and the pharmacist were friends? No, she knew him, but the only time they spoke was when she went in to get a prescription filled. Nevertheless, she remained loyal to this drug store until it finally merged with a chain drug store down the street.

High S's are predictable. You may not like what they're going to do, but at least you know they're going to do it. They're steady and stable, and they'll rarely surprise you. High S's do not like change. Of course, they're capable of change as long as they are given time to adjust and a logical reason to do so. High S's tend to get up, eat, exercise, and go to bed on a well-established schedule. They also tend to arrive and depart the workplace at specific times, regardless of the workload.

I once had a client whose behavior profile measured 100 percent S — as high as he could go on the scale. This gentleman refused to believe it; he was not that predictable, he said. When he got home to his wife, he remarked on the absurdity of the profile. When he awoke the next morning, his wife had already gone to work. On the bathroom mirror he found a note: "1." In the shower he found "2." Number three was by the coffee pot. When he got to seven, he called his wife. "You have the same routine every morning," she said. "I know exactly where you're going to go, what you're going to do, and in what order." The man finally admitted that he probably did, indeed, fit the High S profile.

High S's are logical. They will accept change as long as it's logical. Using strong emotions with the High S is usually unproductive; he wants reasons, in orderly sequence. Don't shoot from the hip when dealing with a High S; instead, think through your plans or actions. Appeal to his sense of logic.

High S's are disciplined. Their time is important to them, and they usually manage it well, doing things on a predictable schedule. If you allow them enough time, you can usually count on them to complete the job in a logical, organized manner.

High S's like harmony. They abhor discord. In fact, they will do whatever they can to ensure that people work together well. Even if they're not directly involved, they may act as an intermediary to settle a conflict.

STRENGTHS OF THE HIGH S

The High S is dependable. You can count on her to do what she says she'll do, no matter to what lengths or pains she must go.

The High S is supportive. A High S will often sacrifice his own interests to support those with whom he inter- acts — his boss, the work team, his family, you. He may also support people you don't agree with.

The High S is a team player. To him, the team is para- mount; the High S may ask that a team decision be put off until an absent member can be consulted. He seldom takes credit for work done, even if he was a key player on the team.

The High S works well with repetition. Work that is repetitive gives her a welcome sense of stability and steadi- ness. She finds comfort in tasks that others find boring or mundane, such as routine paperwork. This aspect of her work usually keeps her managers happy.

The High S follows requests. When you tell him what you want done and how you want it done, he will work diligently to complete the task. If your instructions are not specific enough, however, he may simply wait for further guidance. This frustrates D's and I's, who tend to provide targets rather than road maps.

The High S establishes rapport. She's not quick to make judgments or decisions; instead, she likes to take the time to get acquainted with people and situations. For this reason, her knowledge and understanding of the organi- zation can be a valuable asset.

The High S is organized. She may not get organized as quickly as the D, but she'll be more thorough and logical. I hired a new office manager who was a very High S. Within two months she had the administrative office completely reorganized. One of her suggestions was to move the copier from the break room into the administrative office, on another floor. This very logical change, which had never before occurred to anyone, saved us countless trips up and down the stairs.

The High S is practical. She looks for the obvious or easiest solution. She doesn't see any purpose in making a big fuss about something when it can be handled quietly or avoided.

W hen two of my friends, who are married to each other, dine out together, trouble often follows. Are the steaks overcooked? The husband, a High D, will send his back and demand another, and perhaps even demand a discount for the inconvenience. This is quite embarrassing for his wife, a High S. She'd rather eat it than make a fuss. She just won't come back to that restaurant.

Major Weaknesses of the High S

High S's avoid confrontation. Often they will avoid taking necessary action because the High S simply doesn't want to call someone on the carpet. He'd rather correct an error himself than confront the individual responsible. It's important for the S to understand that a person can be confronted without anger or hurt feelings.

High S's are worriers. Others may see them as whiners, but change is difficult for them. With changes coming faster and faster, today's society often finds worried S's dragging their feet. They can take a long time to make a decision. Compounding this difficulty is their reluctance to hurt anyone's feelings or confront those who don't like their decisions. They tend to sit on the fence until they either fall or get pushed off.

High S's tend to sit on the fence until they either fall or get pushed off.

NEEDS OF THE HIGH S

High S's need appreciation. They don't need a showy public display or fanfare like the I, but quiet appreciation. A typical High S would prefer to get a handwritten note of appreciation in the mail; this way, he can savor the words in private and avoid the embarrassment of being complimented in person. I tell managers to keep a number of cards on hand and use them to thank their High S's privately when they do something noteworthy.

High S's need a steady pace. They don't do well in a volatile, unstable environment. I doubt you will find may High S's working on Wall Street. Of course, everyone needs some change, and the S can handle necessary changes when given good reasons and time to adjust.

High S's like expectations. They want to know what you want them to do, expressed in detailed, step-by-step instructions, so they can measure their performance against your expectations. What, exactly, should be the outcome? When, exactly, do you expect it to be done? High S's don't like surprises.

High S's need closure. They like to know that a job is complete, that the work and time that they've invested have meant something. Only then can they move on to the next thing. They don't like loose ends.

GOAL OF THE HIGH S

The goal of the High S is consistency. He doesn't want any big surprises in his life. Change under his control is acceptable; it's spontaneous external change that is unwelcome.

To successfully implement an organizational change, it's important to give the S as much advance notice as possible. As soon as you know change is coming, tell him. Don't wait until the last minute because you dread telling him or because you're too busy.

Three weeks before it was to happen, I announced at our weekly staff meeting that for four consecutive weeks each staff member would be required to record his activities in fifteen-minute increments. The purpose of this admittedly burdensome project, I said, was to show us how we could better manage our time. Secretly, I knew that no one would enjoy doing this, except one High C who would take pleasure in recording the information accurately.

The following week, I reminded everyone that the project was two weeks away and that next week they would receive the necessary forms. A week later the forms arrived. I allowed time for staff members to ask questions. I noticed that during the final week before we started the project, the High S's in the office were showing discomfort, saying things like "Gee, next week I'd have to write down that I spent this whole fifteen minutes talking."

When the time came to begin our record keeping, the High S's were okay with it. They had three weeks to adjust to the changes. Had I sprung it on them at the last minute, I would have heard great wailing and gnashing of teeth.

EMOTIONS OF THE HIGH S

High S's mask their emotions. Like all humans, of course, they will share their feelings, whether positive or negative, with close friends or family, but to the rest of the world, the High S's emotions are not evident. You might never suspect that a High S is angry with you. The High S considers this a virtue. In his mind, people who show their anger or excitement, as High D's and High I's are prone to do, simply lack self-control.

It's difficult as well to read the High S's body language. Small, subtle movements may mean a great deal. When an

I is excited, you'll see broad, rapid gestures, facial contortions, shifts in posture; the equivalent for an S may be a slight movement of the fingertips.

HOW TO LEAD THE HIGH S

Leaders who clearly explain upcoming changes and allow plenty of time to prepare will work well with High S's. Managers who encourage High S's to contribute during group meetings and involve them in long-term planning help them feel a part of the change. It is important to work with the High S to develop a sequential plan for personal and career growth.

High S's perform best on a few large projects rather than many small projects. They like to be allowed to complete a task uninterrupted, and they don't respond well to managers who are constantly pushing on the accelerator and then slamming on the brakes. Concrete rewards, such as raises, bonuses, and larger offices, are best for motivating the High S.

HOW THE S WANTS TO BE TREATED

Clarify detail. High I's and D's have some difficulty with this because they like to give the bottom line — it's faster and more efficient. The S, however, wants the details in order to see the complete picture. Even though it takes more time, provide clear details rather than generalizations.

Be sincere. If the High S thinks you're being phony, she will disregard your information. High I's probably have more difficulty with this than other styles; the S often sees the I's enthusiasm as artificial. When I speak in public, I can usually spot the High S's in the audience. They are reserved; they don't laugh at my opening witticisms; but when I get to the more serious part of my presentation, they finally jump on board. I've had many of them come up to me afterward and say something to the effect of "I thought at first you were all glitz, but you genuinely are a real person."

Establish trust. Don't try to be too friendly too quickly. Don't tell the High S your life story in the first four minutes — you'll scare him off. If you have a customer who is a High S, know that it's going to take longer to establish a relationship with him. You may find yourself making three or four initial calls rather than one or two. Take the time to gain his respect and trust.

Allow the High S time to decide. Don't rush him or push him. He doesn't respond well to time pressure. Salespeople who tell the High S, "This offer is good today only," will most certainly lose the sale. For the same reasons, I tell managers to give the High S time to adjust to change and time to decide on options.

Stress organization, not change. Show the High S how the changes will make life more efficient, more orderly. Make your presentation logical.

Cite precedent. Don't stress originality; the High S prefers the tried and proven. She doesn't want to be the first — it's too risky. Let her know that the decision does not involve a high risk. Listing precedents and references can help.

Flatter his work effort. Do not flatter the person. Remember that the High S is an introvert and doesn't like being in the spotlight. If you give compliments, praise his work — that is something that can be appreciated.

Provide guarantees. Don't promise what you can't deliver. Let the High S know exactly what you can and cannot do. Make it clear; put it in writing.

Begin with social talk. The High S prefers to spend a few minutes getting to know you before turning to business; many people make the mistake of going directly to the matter at hand. You'll get a lot further with the High S if he knows and trusts you. High S's don't care how much you know until they know how much you care.

Don't assume that the silence means ignorance. With the High S, it may mean he doesn't understand the question, but it may also mean he's composing his answer. Wait five to seven seconds; if he hasn't responded, rephrase the question. Whatever you do, don't give up.

Stress logic. Don't get emotional and make demands; the High S can see right through this, and you'll look like a fool to her.

One of the best ways to begin a conversation with the High S is to ask a StartProbe that begins with "how." This allows her to compose a detailed answer with the information organized logically. Whatever you do, don't begin with closed questions or questions that can be answered with one word. Your goal is to unmask this communicator; you need to get her to talk in order to do that.

Once you get her talking, demonstrate clearly that you're listening. Don't sit there expressionless as a stone statue; use body language and neutral comments to show you're interested. Whatever you do, don't interrupt her.

You can expect a High S to take things to heart. Be careful what you say; think before speaking. You may not know that the High S has been hurt, because he masks his emotions. He may hold it inside forever.

I had two close friends, both High S's, who were married to each other. They were experiencing marital difficulty, and I was often witness to the beginning of an argument. Both would begin dredging up incidents that happened five years or more in the past. This is typical High S behavior: emotionless on the surface, quite capable of holding onto slights, insults, and injuries. These may be played over and over in the mind — not a healthy activity.

Selling to the High S

Don't rush. Go slow. Take the time to earn her trust. Ask her for questions. D's and I's pop out questions as quickly as they think of them, but the S is more reserved. Take the time to thoroughly answer her questions.

Plan your pitch. When you're making a presentation, make it logically and sequentially. Don't provide information randomly or casually.

Provide proof. This is important. Give evidence of what you say, preferably in writing. A list of precedents, or of people or organizations who have used your product, service, or information, will help the High S decide in your favor. Show how your product or service will minimize change and increase efficiency. Remember, he doesn't want to be a pioneer; he wants something that is steady, stable, and sure.

Use a quiet manner. Don't be pushy, loud, or flamboyant. Give the High S time to think and decide. Tell him up front, "I know you want to think about this, so I'm going to leave all this information with you. When would be a good time this week for me to call you?" By taking the pressure off, you earn his trust.

Statements that will motivate the High S to buy could include these:

> "Here's a list of people you can call who have used our service."
>
> "We've been in business fifteen years, so we'll be here when you need us."
>
> "This product is proven. You can rely on it."
>
> "Our guarantee eliminates risk."

ONE ON ONE

About 40 percent of the U.S. population is High S. These Steady types shop for traditional products; they search for security. Don't rush them; let them warm to you. Give them information logically and sequentially. Listening to them and showing that you're interested will bring huge deposits into your people account.

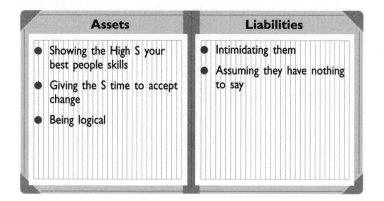

Assets	Liabilities
• Showing the High S your best people skills	• Intimidating them
• Giving the S time to accept change	• Assuming they have nothing to say
• Being logical	

It is thrifty to prepare today
for the wants of tomorrow.

AESOP

*Take time to deliberate; but when the time for action
arrives, stop thinking and go in.*

ANDREW JACKSON

THE COMPLIANT
PERSONALITY

You may get the impression that all the task-oriented introvert wants is to be left alone. Although Compliant behavior types do work well on their own, they also recognize the need to communicate. They want information from you, and when you don't have it, you may learn to your chagrin that talk is not cheap. Being unprepared for the High C can cost you both time and self-esteem.

One of our lead trainers loves information. I noticed when we started traveling together that he always carried more luggage than I did. His suitcases were filled not with clothing but with files and references that this High C felt he needed in case someone wanted more detailed information. (I sometimes jokingly referred to it as his traveling reference library.) When we entered a seminar room, he would methodically set up his references.

At one seminar, a participant asked for the percentage breakdown by gender on a particular behavior trait. "There's no significant difference," I said. "It's approximately 14 percent, give or take one percent between the genders." As soon as the words were out of my mouth, I saw the alarm in my co-presenter's eyes. I had committed the unforgivable sin: I had generalized or guesstimated statistics. Riffling through his files, he quickly found the exact numbers: 13 percent were females, he informed us, and 15 percent were males.

The participant looked at me. I shrugged. "Like I said," I said, "about 14 percent." It was good for a laugh — and a good opportunity to talk about differences between behavior styles and the ways people handle information.

TRAITS OF THE HIGH C

High C's are compliant. They respect rules and regulations, law and order, and tend to abide by them. They are also very conscientious. Long after others have tired of the details, the High C keeps on going.

High C's are cautious. They like low-risk situations. They are very careful about what they're doing.

High C's are competent. They love information, and they love sharing that information with other interested parties.

High C's are calculating. They think things through before they say them. They are unlikely to say something off the cuff or to be spontaneous.

High C's are critical thinkers. They love to be correct. They spend more time than most gathering information and thinking things through to ensure that they are correct. This sometimes causes others to see them as self-righteous, but the High C's goal is not to be superior to other people — just to be right.

High C's are control freaks. They don't necessarily set out to control you; they just want to keep the event, project, or situation under their control. This is their way of ensuring that the quality or the result meets their high standards.

High C's are conformists. The tried and true is important to them, and yet they're often looking for ways to improve it. Your opinions mean very little to a High C, but if you prove your point with new information, you can persuade him to change his mind.

High C's are consistent. You can predict what their response is going to be. You may not like it, but you probably won't be surprised.

STRENGTHS OF THE HIGH C

The High C is highly organized. When you walk into her office, it may look disorganized because she's not necessarily a neat freak like a High D. However, she'll be able to put her hand on any piece of paper you request. This organization ability extends to her projects and plans. She's a great list maker, and she lists everything. This sounds like a wonderful trait, but remember, it takes a lot of time. If you want something done quickly, the High C is not the person to give it to.

The High C is critical. He's excellent at analyzing information. If you allow him to tear your idea apart, he'll make it stronger. Some people cannot handle criticism of their work and are sensitive to this trait. Sometimes a person wants the High C to evaluate, and sometimes a person just wants to share her pride in her work; the High C needs to understand the difference.

The High C likes detail. He is fascinated by information and surprised that others may want to skip over the fine print and look at the bottom line.

R ecently, while working on a writing project, I called up one of our researchers who is a High C and asked him whether a particular phrase was from the Bible. I wanted a simple yes or no, but he told me he would call me back. I waited impatiently; I was sure he knew the answer. Why was he stalling?

Ten minutes later he called with a list of verses in which this phrase could be found. I was overwhelmed with information. After he read the second reference, I said, "Whoa, whoa, whoa. You've answered my question. You've given me more information than I need. I simply wanted to know if this was a biblical reference. Thank you very much." I think he was actually disappointed that I didn't want to hear all seventeen verses that he had located.

The High C is cautious. He's not quick to jump on the bandwagon, a trait that sometimes makes him seem like a wet blanket when others are excited over a new project. The High C's caution often prevents costly mistakes; however, it can also keep him from taking advantage of sudden opportunities. I know one High C who was 98 percent sure of a decision but spent an additional two weeks so he could be 98.7 percent sure — a delay that cost him the account.

The High C is logical. Think of Data and Mr. Spock from the *Star Trek* series. The way to get the High C to change his mind is to give him information and present it logically. Save your emotions — they won't work on the High C. In fact, he has little respect for anyone who deals with everything emotionally.

The High C is task-oriented. It's not that he hates people, it's that his focus, like that of the High D, is on getting the job done. But he's also an introvert; like the S, he wants to do it by himself, and without a lot of attention.

The High C is a perfectionist. Being correct is very important; the job isn't done until it's done perfectly. The High C agonizes over minor flaws that 86 percent of the population will never notice. This eats up time and can hurt productivity.

Major Weaknesses of the High C

High C's find it hard to be flexible. They are not very spontaneous. The typical High C wants more information than other types. This adherence to data makes them seem rigid and inflexible, reluctant to generalize and get to the bottom line.

High C's can be slow to respond. Because they tend to be perfectionists, they take longer to complete projects and are more likely to miss deadlines.

Needs of the High C

The C needs time. Like the other introvert, the S, the High C needs to gather information, think, and make certain she's right. When she's put under a time constraint,

---

My husband Ken and I got new cars about fourteen months apart. Ken, being a High C, immediately came home and read his automobile manual from cover to cover. Mine stayed tucked away in the glove compartment.

One day as my son and I were leaving the house, my son complained that every time he got out to close the driveway gate, the back door of the car locked itself. "I'm sure there's a way to undo that," I said. "Mommie hasn't read the instructions to this car yet." I'd had the car three months.

THE COMPLIANT PERSONALITY

she can get quite nervous. Her greatest fear is that she'll make a mistake.

The High C needs information. This is, of course, her greatest need. She doesn't want the overview — she wants the details. She reads the footnotes. When she goes to a movie, she stays for the credits.

To provide him with something more suitable for traveling, a High C in our office was given authorization to replace his desktop computer with a new laptop. It took him about six weeks of fact finding, but he eventually purchased a computer of an unfamiliar brand. According to his research it was state of the art, but it arrived afflicted with a virus and other problems that rendered it unusable. After weeks of getting reports that he was still "working on his computer," I finally insisted that he box it up and ship it back to the manufacturer before the thirty-day satisfaction guarantee expired. This High C found it very hard to admit that the computer he had researched so thoroughly could be so flawed.

The High C needs low-risk situations. When you ask her to take a chance, she gets very uncomfortable. She's most secure making decisions that she has researched thoroughly. Most people hesitate before making a large investment or a major decision, but a High C will sometimes agonize over a decision for so long that, suffering from "the paralysis of analysis," she simply fails to decide.

High C's need written procedures. They perform best when they know the exact steps required to accomplish a task. They may improve on these procedures, but without them the C may not function well.

GOAL OF THE HIGH C

The goal of the High C is to be right. She is likely to know more about things that interest her than other behavioral styles; some High C's carry that information in their head, others in their briefcase. It's difficult for a C to admit that she's wrong, so she does her best to have all the facts on her side.

EMOTIONS OF THE HIGH C

The most obvious emotion of the High C is fear. He fears being wrong. To be correct — in some cases, perfect — is very important to the High C. Sometimes this keeps the High C from taking advantage of fleeting opportunities.

HOW TO LEAD THE HIGH C

Involve the High C in defining standards, policies, and procedures, as well as in implementing them. Make sure job requirements are fully and clearly stated in writing. Set goals that are attainable, but set deadlines and stick to them if possible.

Planning is a key strength of this task-oriented introvert. A leader who involves the High C in long-term planning will reap benefits. During meetings, encourage the C to speak up, especially in his areas of expertise. He's not comfortable with spontaneity or surprises, so give him time to plan a response. One way to do this is to state a question before you need the answer: "Bob, in just a minute I'm going to ask you about the engineering plans, but first let me talk about . . ."

The High C may benefit from training in people skills. Make sure the training is informative; the High C loves information.

How a C Wants to Be Treated

Be patient. Don't expect quick decisions. High C's will not be rushed. You will only frustrate yourself if you try to push them into a quick decision.

Be organized. Go to meetings with all your ducks in a row. Bring new information to add to the C's knowledge; present it logically and sequentially, and have it in writing so the C can assimilate it later. Weed out all flaws in your logic before you present it. If you show confusion, the C will not respect the information and will be slower in completing the work or coming to a decision.

Provide details. Do not generalize with a High C. In particular, D's and I's need to temper their tendency to skip to the bottom line.

Stick to the facts. Getting emotional is not logical, and it gets you nowhere with a C. High D's in particular need to strive not to intimidate the C.

Choose words carefully. High C's are not skilled at reading between the lines. Don't hint at anything; say what you mean. If your High C boss asks you how you feel about the change in the project, don't look down at your shoes and mumble, "Okay." He will not read between the lines. He heard you say okay, and he believes you meant it.

Show the High C how to minimize risk. Don't ask her to gamble, but since there's almost always an element of risk in any decision, you can help the High C perform by planning for contingencies. She'll appreciate your foresight and your attention to detail.

Expect tough questions. Come prepared. The High C will ask questions on obscure details and issues that have never occurred to you. If you don't know the answer, don't fake it; say, "I don't have the information to answer that question, but I'll get it for you by four o'clock." Then, even if you don't have a complete answer, follow through and report back to him by four o'clock.

Be direct. Don't dodge the issues; face the High C head on. He's pretty thick skinned; you're not likely to hurt his feelings.

Set deadlines and stick to them. Don't leave projects open ended. Because the High C pursues the unattainable goal of perfection, she'll keep working on the job as long as you let her. Once you allow the High C to miss a deadline, she may infer that completeness has priority over urgency. This feeds her fear that being rushed means being wrong. To avoid unpleasant last-minute surprises — "I can't possibly get this done" — check on her progress at regular intervals. Intermediate deadlines can help.

Give him space. A handshake is fine; a too-long handshake or a slap on the back may be inappropriate. In a business setting, give the High C at least three feet of personal space. (In a personal situation, of course, the High C can enjoy human contact as readily as anyone.)

Ask questions. A High C prefers open-ended questions; closed questions don't allow him to give you all the information he feels is vital. Unless you want excessive detail, however, you should focus your questions to address a particular issue. I've even advised people to preface a question with "Can you briefly tell me . . ." or "Can you tell me in twenty-five words or less . . ."

SELLING TO THE HIGH C

Take your time; don't rush. Make sure you answer all questions thoroughly. Bring additional written material with you, such as product brochures, for the High C to digest after the initial sales meeting.

Stick to business. Don't spend time trying to warm up the High C. She's not at the sales meeting to make friends, but to decide which product or service she wishes to purchase.

Document your information. Conduct research before the sales meeting so that you can offer the High C proof of what you say in writing or through references.

Find ways to minimize risk. The High C likes guarantees. Show him how his investment will be protected. Letters of recommendations from satisfied customers can be useful; the High C will read every word.

Present a well-thought-out proposal. Don't throw one together at the last minute. Your proposal needs to be neat, concise, and orderly. It should also be thorough; for the High C, this usually means longer and more detailed.

Statements that would spur the High C to buy from you might include the following:

"The quality of our service is detailed in this brochure."

"Once you've examined the facts, you'll be comfortable with this product."

"Here is all the information you'll need to investigate which of our products are right for you."

JUST THE FACTS

The 14 percent of the U.S. population that are High C's like to buy proven products and services. They seek information. Make sure you give it to them, or you'll pay the high cost of misunderstanding at work and at home.

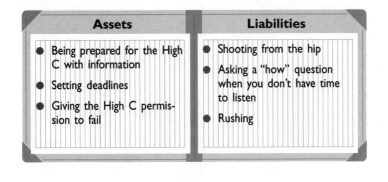

Assets	Liabilities
● Being prepared for the High C with information	● Shooting from the hip
● Setting deadlines	● Asking a "how" question when you don't have time to listen
● Giving the High C permission to fail	● Rushing

He who is slow in promising is always the most faithful in performing.

JEAN JACQUES ROUSSEAU

It is best to learn as we go,
not go as we have learned.

LESLIE JEANNE SAHLER

THE INTERPLAY
OF STYLES

By now you should
have a good idea of
the strengths, weak-
nesses, preferences, and
tendencies of each behavior type. It takes time to learn all
the subtleties of anyone you meet, and you should never
make snap judgments that might prejudice the way you
perceive and deal with the individual.

It's interesting to note, however, that you can often get an early signal of a person's general behavior style by listening to the way he asks for information. The diagram below shows five examples of how the four basic behavior types might ask you the same question.

D	I
1. What's the cost?	1. If I purchase from you, what discount will you give me?
2. Is this new?	2. How is this model different from the other ones?
3. I think this will work, don't you?	3. What do you think?
4. Have you ever managed before?	4. What experience in management do you have?
5. Do you have a better suggestion?	5. What suggestions can you offer?

C	S
1. Exactly what is included in your price?	1. I'm happy with my current supplier. What is your price?
2. How did the research company test this new product?	2. I don't trust new products. I want one that I know works.
3. Can you provide the details in writing so I can determine if it will work?	3. Do you think this will really work?
4. Do you have a copy of your management philosophy?	4. How long have you managed in each position?
5. What is your suggestion, and exactly how would it be implemented?	5. Do you have a minor suggestion that will improve efficiency without disrupting the whole procedure?

Notice how D's come straight to the point and use few words; they let you know who's in charge. I's ask open questions and try to engage you in conversation; they want to get to know you. S's hesitate before asking for information; their discomfort with or reluctance to change is obvious. C's use words like "precisely," "exactly," "details"; their questions are tough and will probably require you to bring written material or do additional research.

It will come as no surprise to you that some styles interact better than others. The chart shows, in general, how well various pairings are likely to work on initial contact. The greater the overlap, the better they'll get along.

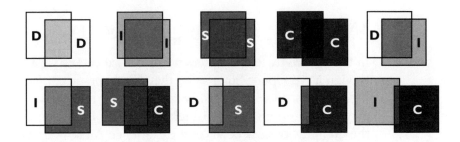

Most people interact reasonably well with another person of similar style. When two I's meet, they feel as though they've found a long-lost friend. D's and I's get along quite well, too. High C's, because they are introverted and task oriented, have the least success fitting in with others, in particular with extroverts.

This does not mean that a C should not interact with an I, nor a D with an S; in the workplace, avoidance leads to disaster. What it does mean is that these combinations have to adapt more, make the effort to communicate successfully with each other, and — because talk is not cheap — keep making deposits in their people accounts.

TEST YOURSELF ON STYLE

Another quick way to determine an individual's behavioral style is to ask yourself two questions:

- Is this person task oriented or people oriented?
- Is this person an extrovert or an introvert?

Use this formula, you can probably determine the person's primary behavior style. It won't give you the complete picture, but it's a beginning.

WHEN STYLES ARE BLENDED

In the preceding four chapters we discussed each style as though it were pure, but it's rare that a real person can be described in these terms. To believe that any real personality can be described in a single dimension is to ignore the complexity of genetics and experience. Most people embody a blend of behavioral styles, of which two are usually prominent. The specific combination and its nuances are what make each person unique and interesting. Below, in general terms, is what you might expect to find in each blend.

D/I: When a High D is also a High I, you have a confirmed extrovert. This person wants to lead! She's a quick decision maker who initiates change and handles it well. Her

D   I   S   C

balance between task and people skills can make her very productive. Her challenge is to remember to listen. The D in her brings impatience; the I compels her to talk and to be the center of attention.

Ask her "what" questions to get information without making her feel manipulated. The D in her may be too impatient to answer a "how" question, though the I may tend to give you more answer than you asked for.

D/S: When a High D is also a High S, you can have either a very balanced person or Dr. Jekyll/Mr. Hyde. When balanced, this individual's tendency to confront is tempered by his people skills; he knows when to take command and when to listen. You can expect him to be logical, organized, and good at managing his time. When his behavior styles conflict, you may sense two different people in him. For instance, his need for change may be continually at war with his need to hold onto the familiar. Interacting with him then becomes challenging: you may not know which one came to work today. Plan your comments carefully; appearing disorganized, giving estimates in place of facts, and being careless with your people skills can cost you.

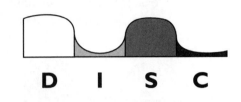

D/C: This individual is all business. She can easily direct others, yet may wish to be left alone. Uncomfortable with small talk, she can feel awkward in social settings and have difficulty with relationships. Her internal conflict is often a time issue: her need to be decisive runs up against her compulsion to be accurate. When you communicate with her, choose your words carefully; she may not have developed the skills to read your body language and tone of voice. If you're high on the I or S scales, be ready to protect your self-esteem. Don't take her comments personally. Remember, she's task oriented in the extreme.

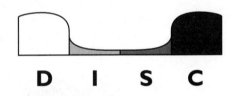

I/S: This combination is definitely a people person. He puts people first, sometimes acting as an extrovert and other times as a member of a team. Others will do things for him just because they like him. His inner conflict is between his competing urges to be spontaneous and orderly — a nice balance if he has the insight to exploit it. However, he may find confrontations difficult, which may cause problems for him as a manager. If

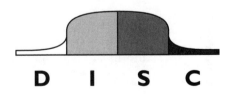

you have this blend, take care to plan your corrective actions and keep them focused on the task, not the person.

I/C: This blend of styles, like the D/S, can be either very balanced or very difficult to read. She can be outgoing at times, reclusive at others: "Guess who I am now!" Optimally,

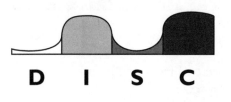

D   I   S   C

she can balance her creative temperament against her practicality. The inner conflict between being correct and being creative can mean that her wonderful ideas never come to fruition. To communicate with this blend, appeal to her warmth and be prepared to supply the details for her curious mind. If this blend describes you, learn to set deadlines for yourself.

S/C: This blended style prefers the support role. He feels intimidated when asked to step into the limelight. The combination of task and people orientation can work well

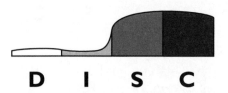

D   I   S   C

for him as a manager; he feels more comfortable with confrontation when he has valid information on his side. The same combination can, however, lead to indecisiveness; which to focus on? As an introvert, he is naturally reluctant to speak. You may find "what" and "how" TripleProbes useful in getting him to open up. When he does, silence yourself and listen. If this is your blend, you'll probably find it easier to share information than opinion.

Take a few minutes and list people you know by their styles. After you've done so, ask yourself which styles you find most challenging to interact with. What adjustments do you need to make?

THE POWER OF STYLES

Because each person is unique, identifying a predominant behavior style cannot give us a complete picture of the individual. It can, however, give us some guidelines to help us communicate more effectively. To understand more deeply a person's needs, dreams, motivations, and actions, you need a more comprehensive profile. For more information on how to obtain one, see page 254.

Some would say, "The more you know, the more you know you don't know." I like to think that the more I know, the more prepared I will be. As Aristotle said, "Knowledge is power." I might offer Aristotle an amplification: "Applied knowledge is power."

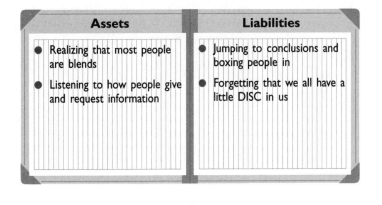

Assets	Liabilities
• Realizing that most people are blends • Listening to how people give and request information	• Jumping to conclusions and boxing people in • Forgetting that we all have a little DISC in us

He who knows others is learned;
he who knows himself is wise.

LAO TZU

My problem lies in reconciling my gross habits
with my net income!

ERROL FLYNN

THE RETURN ON
YOUR INVESTMENT

hen you make a finan-
cial investment in
stocks, bonds, mutual
funds, or a savings ac-
count, you can see the return on your investment in your
monthly financial statement. If you've invested well, the
return is positive, which instills in you a feeling of satisfaction. When you make the Four Deposits for Balance,
what return should you expect?

Expect a greater peace within yourself through the application of a positive attitude. There is tremendous personal power in knowing you control your attitude. It brings a balance and harmony to your soul that allows you to handle the everyday ups and downs. People may start commenting that you look healthier and happier. Expect people to exclaim that they just don't know how you do it all.

Expect to get smarter through the habit of genuinely listening to other people. Unless you plan to master mind reading, listening is your best route to understanding people. When you truly understand what the other person is striving to say, you connect. It clicks.

Expect to receive more respect through the combined efforts of listening first and then planning your response. This greatly reduces mistakes. When you model the ability to listen and then speak with care, you'll find more people listen to you. They'll want to emulate your behavior. Your statements will not get lost in the noise of idle chatter but will stand solid in their minds.

Expect to eliminate unrealistic expectations of others through understanding their behavioral style, reading their body language, and discovering the secrets of their voice. You'll find that people don't surprise you much anymore. This allows you to be prepared and prevent misunderstandings.

Expect to save time because you communicate effectively the first time and don't have to go back and fix it. Conversations for tasks and meetings will be shorter.

Expect to feel more organized because communication is clear and you can actually see where you're headed. Clearing the mind is like straightening a cluttered desk; it feels good.

Expect people close to you to notice a difference. To forestall suspicion, tell them what you're doing. When you change, they will automatically change how they interact with you. People in general are resistant to change. When you share with them what you're doing and how you're doing it, they feel less threatened, less manipulated, less fearful.

Expect to get excited when you derive success from making the Four Deposits for Balance. Feel the pride in knowing that you've accomplished something worthwhile through purposeful effort. Celebrate!

Expect to build stronger relationships with the people you hold dear. Expect to have a meaningful conversation with your child, spouse, parent, or friend. You'll experience the warmth that begins within your chest and radiates throughout your body. Your eyes may moisten with the emotion of truly connecting with this precious person.

Expect to like yourself better. With the positive feedback from others in addition to your new track record, expect contentment. You may catch yourself smiling for no particular reason.

Expect to make fewer mistakes, which saves time, money, and relationships. Your confidence will soar!

When we make a financial investment, there are times when, in spite of our efforts to study and invest wisely, we lose funds. Can we expect similar results when we make the Four Deposits for Balance? I say no. I say this with confidence. I guarantee it. How can I assure you that you cannot lose?

Remember the first deposit: Set your own attitude and altitude. Regardless of what a person says or does, you still have control of your attitude through the use of the Public and Private Attitude Plans. It may take concentrated work; most worthwhile things do. Others may knock you down, but with the first deposit they do not have the power to keep you down unless you relinquish your personal power.

Remember, talk is not cheap! What happens if you fail to make deposits? You will pay the consequence. It will cost you money, time, relationships, and self-esteem. Identify what you've done, correct it, and resolve to do better. Don't spend precious time worrying. Spend that time planning. Instead of "I should have . . ." tell yourself, "Next time I will . . ."

I encourage you to practice before you really need it. A tennis player doesn't wait until Wimbledon to practice serves. Begin now. Tell people you're striving to be a better listener and communicator. Ask them to give you feedback. When the stressful times come, you'll be ready.

Making the Four Deposits for Balance regularly will yield compound interest. Your benefits will grow beyond your expectations. Make these investments with your boss and co-workers and watch your career soar. Make these investments with your loved ones and reap the reward of giving the most precious gift. Most of all, make these investments in yourself, because it all starts with you. You can make the difference.

Success comes in cans;
failure comes in cannots.

ANONYMOUS

BIBLIOGRAPHY

Beckwith, Harry. *Selling the Invisible: A Field Guide to Modern Marketing.* New York: Warner Books, 1997.

Berne, Eric. *Games People Play.* New York: Grove Press, 1964.

Bonnstetter, Bill, Judy Suiter, and Randy Widrick. *The Universal Language DISC.* Scottsdale, Ariz.: Target Training International, Ltd., 1993.

Burley-Allen, Madelyn. *Listening: The Forgotten Skill (A Self-Teaching Guide).* New York: John Wiley & Sons, Inc., 1982.

Buzan, Tony. *Make the Most of Your Mind.* New York: Linden Press, 1984.

Buzan, Tony. *Use Both Sides of Your Brain.* New York: Plume, 1991.

Buzan, Tony. *Use Your Perfect Memory.* New York: Plume, 1991.

Carnegie, Dale. *How to Win Friends and Influence People.* New York: Simon & Schuster, 1937.

Conn, Charles Paul. *The Winner's Circle.* Old Tappan, N.J.: Revell, 1979.

Cooper, Morton. *Change Your Voice, Change Your Life: A Quick, Simple Plan for Finding and Using Your Natural, Dynamic Voice.* New York: Barnes & Noble, 1985.

Cousins, Norman. *Anatomy of an Illness as Perceived by the Patient: Reflections on Healing and Regeneration.* New York: Norton, 1979.

Covey, Stephen R. *First Things First: To Live, to Love, to Learn, to Leave a Legacy.* New York: Simon & Schuster, 1994.

Covey, Stephen R. *The Seven Habits of Highly Effective People: Restoring the Character Ethic.* Thorndike, Me.: G.K. Hall, 1997.

Ebel, Kenneth E. *Achieving Excellence in Business: A Practical Guide to the Total Quality Transformation Process.* Milwaukee: ASQC Quality Press, 1991.

Fulghum, Robert. *It Was on Fire When I Lay Down on It.* New York: Villard Books, 1989.

Giblin, Les. *How to Have Confidence and Power in Dealing with People.* Englewood Cliffs, N.J.: Prentice-Hall, 1956.

Gozdz, Kazimierz (ed). *Community Building: Renewing Spirit & Learning in Business.* San Francisco: Sterling & Stone, Inc., 1995.

Gray, John. *Men Are from Mars, Women Are from Venus: A Practical Guide for Improving Communication and Getting What You Want in Your Relationships.* New York: HarperCollins, 1992.

Gray, John. *What You Feel You Can Heal: A Guide for Enriching Relationships.* Mill Valley, Calif: Heart Pub., 1994.

Harvey, Eric L., and Alexander Lucia. *Walk the Talk . . . and Get the Results You Want.* Dallas: Treeview Pub., 1993.

Hawken, Paul. *Growing a Business.* New York: Simon & Schuster, 1987.

Herrmann, Ned. *The Creative Brain.* Lake Lure, N.C.: Brain Books, 1988.

Isachsen, Olaf, and Linda V. Berens. *Working Together: A Personality-Centered Approach to Management.* Coronado, Calif: Neworld Management Press, 1988.

Jung, Carl Gustav. *Psychological Types.* Princeton, N.J.: Princeton University Press, 1976.

Kenley, Joan. *Voice Power.* New York: Dodd, Mead, 1988.

Linklater, Kristen. *Freeing the Natural Voice.* New York: Drama Book Specialists, 1976.

Lorayne, Harry, and Jerry Lucas. *The Memory Book.* New York: Ballantine, 1974.

Mandino, Og. *The Greatest Salesman in the World.* New York: Phoenix Press, 1986.

Marston, William. *Emotions of Normal People.* Minneapolis: Persona Press, 1979.

McGee-Cooper, Ann. *Time Management for Unmanageable People.* New York: Bantam Books, 1994.

McGee-Cooper, Ann. *You Don't Have to Go Home from Work Exhausted! The Energy Engineering Approach.* New York: Bantam, 1992.

Miller, James B. *The Corporate Coach.* New York: St. Martin's Press, 1993.

Miller, Robert B., and Stephen E. Heiman. *Conceptual Selling: The Revolutionary System for Face-to-Face Selling Used by America's Best Companies.* New York: Warner Books, 1987.

Nierenberg, Gerard I. *The Art of Negotiating: Psychological Strategies for Gaining Advantageous Bargains.* New York: Hawthorn Books, 1977.

Patterson, Miles L. (ed). *Journal of Nonverbal Behavior.* New York: Human Sciences Press, Inc., n.d.

Peters, Tom. *Thriving on Chaos: A Handbook for Management Revolution.* New York: Knopf, 1987.

Pierce, Howard J. *The Owner's Manual for the Brain: Everyday Applications from Mind-Brain Research,* 2nd ed. Austin: Bard Press, 1999. (1st ed. published by Leornian Press, 1994.)

Polhemus, Ted. *The Body Reader: Social Aspects of the Human Body.* New York: Pantheon Books, 1978.

Robbins, Anthony. *Awaken the Giant Within: How to Take Immediate Control of Your Mental, Emotional, Physical & Financial Destiny!* New York: Simon & Schuster, 1992.

Rohm, Robert A. *Positive Personality Profiles: "D-I-S-C-OVER" Personality Insights to Understand Yourself . . . and Others!* Atlanta: Personality Insights, Inc., 1996.

Schwartz, David. *The Magic of Thinking Big.* New York: Simon & Schuster, 1987.

Siegel, Bernie S. *Love, Medicine & Miracles: Lessons Learned About Self-Healing from a Surgeon's Experience with Exceptional Patients.* New York: Harper & Row, 1986.

Smalley, Gary, & John Trent. *The Language of Love: A Powerful Way to Maximize Insight, Intimacy, and Understanding.* Pomona, Calif: Focus on the Family Pub., 1991.

Swenson, Richard A. *Margin: How to Create the Emotional, Physical, Financial & Time Reserves You Need.* Colorado Springs: NavPress, 1992.

Tannen, Deborah. *You Just Don't Understand: Women and Men in Conversation.* New York: William Morrow and Company, Inc., 1990.

Tobias, Cynthia Ulrich. *The Way They Learn: How to Discover and Teach to Your Child's Strengths.* Colorado Springs: Focus on the Family Pub., 1994.

Tobias, Cynthia Ulrich. *The Way We Work: A Practical Approach for Dealing with People on the Job.* Dallas: Focus on the Family Pub., 1995.

Walton, Donald. *Are You Communicating? You Can't Manage Without It.* New York: McGraw-Hill, Inc., 1989.

Whitmore, John. *Coaching for Performance: A Practical Guide to Growing Your Own Skills.* London: Nicholas Brealy Pub., 1994.

Zigler, Zig. *Over the Top.* Nashville: Thomas Nelson, 1994.

INDEX

About TLC

TLC, Talk Listen Communicate, LLC, has a history of creating positive and permanent change, an accomplishment praised by our clients. We have achieved this distinction because of our commitment to identifying and understanding the needs and desires of our clients, and because of the unique combination of methods and approaches that we employ. For example:

- Our sales process focus is based on the concept of partnership, including helping clients understand their unique needs and plan the approach to fulfilling those needs.

- Our individual and group training programs are tailored to the client's specific needs and circumstances, including services that are designed to start the client on the path to change when immediate resources do not permit a direct pursuit of the desired outcome.

- Our trainers, coaches, and consultants are required to complete extensive training programs and pass a series of tests before they are qualified to provide services.

Our training programs are designed to create and reinforce change in the participants, including

- profiles of participants to help them better understand themselves,

- skill practice with video and audio taping of practice sessions,

- materials and tapes for use in self-improvement,

● time for participants to apply their new skills with discussion of their performance,

● small groups with individual coaching sessions, and

● periodic individual coaching sessions and group reunions following completion of the training program to reinforce previous training, promote ongoing self-development, and extend the scope of previous training.

For information on

● Seminars
● Individual training
● Coaching
● Speakers
● Products
● Behavioral profiles

please contact

TLC, Talk Listen Communicate, LLC

842 South Germantown Road

Chattanooga, TN 37412

1-888-BECAUSE

fax: 423-624-4365

e-mail: tlc@byac.com

website: www.byac.com